LEAD GENERATION FOR

WATER

QUALITY DEALERS

2019 Edition

REV UP YOUR LEAD GENERATION

PROGRAM AND DRIVE MORE LEADS

INTO YOUR DEALERSHIP

DALE "DATADALE" FILHABER

A few of my colleagues asked me why I was updating Lead Generation for Water Quality Dealers. After all, this is the third edition.

The truth is that the world of marketing moves so quickly.

SEO techniques that were all the rage 2 years are passé now. Direct mail is back, offering a unique digital component with Informed Delivery. In terms of social media, while Facebook may be peaking, Instagram is on the rise.

The mobile sector continues to explode. We use our phones for much more than communication. Is your company website optimized for mobile search? Have you started to consider how your Dealership can be found via voice search? And, what about video? If you're not using video yet – well, you better get on board.

For 2019, Omni-Channel Marketing is the new catchphrase, stressing the importance of an all-encompassing message regardless of marketing channel. While we still use many of the same media channels for our outreach, the rationale behind it has changed.

In 2019, the key word is Trust. People buy from businesses they trust. How do they come to trust you if they don't know you? You need a comprehensive Engagement Marketing program that hits all the high notes and falls within your budget.

Millennials. In sheer numbers, they surpass Baby Boomers. Are they the big customer now? Will they be tomorrow? We know that Millennials are highly loyal to brands they like. Back to trust. How do you develop a lasting relationship with this critical market segment? You need to develop a strategy for them within your engagement marketing plan.

Health. The Baby Boomer mantra is "as long as you have your health". Boomers know from experience that to live a good life, you need to stay healthy. Boomers are taking direct responsibility for their health with exercise, vitamins, eating better and drinking good quality water. If you are targeting Boomers, health is an overarching concern.

Women. Women control 85% of the discretionary income in the United States and are the decision makers when it comes to household products and the overall health of the family. This year's edition includes a section on Marketing Water Quality Products to Women. You need to speak to her with the right voice and message if you want to generate a response.

Sustainability. One of the most compelling reasons for buying a water filtration system is saving the planet. This is cornerstone content in the water quality industry. Being involved with sustainability lifts a company's reputation and status. Many consumers strongly prefer to do business with companies they view as socially & environmentally responsible.

The world does not stay still. New trends and innovative technology impact our marketing channels unceasingly and businesses that want to stay relevant and profitable have to constantly learn new tricks.

I hope you enjoy Lead Generation for Water Quality Dealers – 2019 edition and learn a few new tricks that help you bring more leads into your dealership.

Table of Contents

Prologue

Every Water Quality Dealership needs to develop a results-oriented lead generation program that brings quality prospects into their business on an on-going basis.

Lead Generation is not an event. It is a well-thought out, multi-faceted plan that takes into consideration your goals, your budget, your resources and your brand.

You will not generate leads with a one-time direct mailing or e-blast. A business needs to be committed to an on-going program to flourish. And, since there are many different techniques of Lead Generation, a business owner will need to be well-versed in several to be successful.

I was at a RainSoft Dealer convention a few years ago and one of the dealers stood up and announced that he used 17 different sources for his lead generation. Different strokes for different folks, he explained. He is my hero. He understands that you need to cast a wide net to bring different types of people into your lead pipeline. No Dealership can survive on a single lead source or using a single channel for their lead generation.

For 2019, think how you can develop relationships with your customers and prospects, selecting the right marketing channels that enable interaction and develop trust.

We all know that the constantly changing and evolving marketing landscape makes it hard to keep up with the latest trends and technology.

This book was written for business owners and marketing managers who want to stay on top of the curve and insure that there is an on-going, steady stream of leads filtering into their Dealership's lead pipeline.

The next few chapters will be looking at developing an effective lead generation program by defining top prospects, examining both Outbound & Inbound strategies, reviewing the top lead generation channels, learning how to calculate costs, understanding the options for testing & tweaking and exploring an integrated approach with an eye towards increasing ROI.

And much of this can be done with a limited budget.

Before we can begin your journey into Lead Generation for Water Dealers and learn about the different strategies, channels or marketing techniques, let's talk about your brand, because it all starts there.

Chapter 1.

Branding

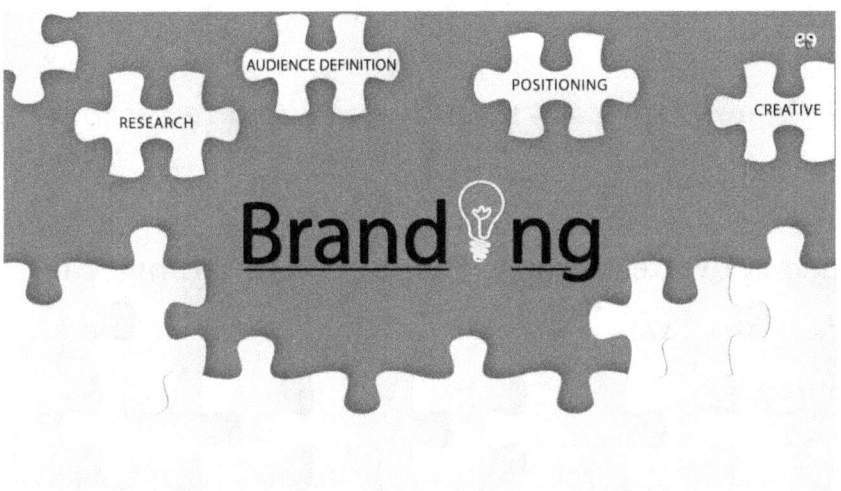

Everyone talks about branding, but what does it really mean to you – as a Water Quality Dealer?

Branding is a concept that extends far beyond the marketing of the "brand name". A company's brand represents their market identity—who they are, what they do, what kind of quality they provide, their reputation for trustworthiness. Because of this, brand marketing is important to nearly every business, from those selling breakfast cereals, to those developing new technologies, to those providing logistic support to other businesses.

A brand name instantly informs customers about a company's reputation, enabling them to trust the quality of the product or service that a business offers. The very mention of the brand name (or the sight of the brand logo) calls up all of a customer's experiences and perceptions of a business—good and bad. Here are a few things you need to consider:

Brand Name - Is it easy to pronounce and remember? Does it sound current with the times?

Let's use EcoWater as an example. It is a strong brand name; includes the word "water" along with a nod to the environment.

In today's culture, the environment can be a real hot button for people, which keeps the brand current.

Brand Equity - Brand equity, by definition, is the real value of a brand name for an organization's products or services. Establishing brand equity is essential because brands are known to be strong influencers of critical business outcomes. Does your brand convey value? How long has your brand been around? Is your dealership known by the brand name?

In the Water Industry, many dealerships do not take advantage of the power that comes with being a dealership for an established brand.

This also speaks to the companies and manufacturer that offer Dealerships. It's time for the national marketing management to make sure they are up-to-par with their brand equity since marketing is a big piece of what the dealers are buying. If you have dealers who are not using your brand name, you need to ask yourself why.

Tagline - Do you have two or three words that pay off your brand name?

Example: *RainSoft, Taking the Worry Out of Water Since 1953*

If you don't have a tagline, you should create one. Sometimes, just refreshing your tagline will be enough to breathe new life into your brand. There is no reason why a dealership cannot personalize their firm by adding a few solid words as well as their location.

Example*: Hague Quality Water of Kansas City, Top Distributor for the 14th consecutive year*

Logo - Is it modern? Are you using colors that bring out the desired emotion of your customer?

There are many studies about the psychology of color. Yellow exudes happiness and excitement; the color blue conveys loyalty, dependability and trust. Click here for the link to my favorite article about the psychology of color.

Unique Selling Proposition - What makes you different – better – than your competition? Is it product, service, knowledge, years in business?

Many Dealers provide lots of home products. Some dealerships market themselves as a one-stop shop for environmental services for the home, including air quality systems, generators, energy efficient HVAC systems, windows & doors, and tankless water heaters.

Other dealerships may stress the fact that Water Quality is the only product they offer. Still other dealerships highlight their community involvement and years in business. Many dealerships highlight the fact that they are family owned and operated.

> **TIP:**
> *Consider a brainstorming session with your staff to discuss your dealerships' Unique Selling Proposition. You may get some great feedback.*

Brand Emotion - Does your brand reflect what you are known for, or would like to be known for?

Great brands aim for customers' hearts. One of the keys to building customer loyalty is invoking emotion.

It's no secret that the highest volume photo genres on Facebook and You-Tube are babies, puppies, dogs & cats and shots invoking love. These make us feel good, we smile. Can these fit in with your unique selling proposition?

Your Story - Stories differentiate you from your competitors. With so many marketing messages bombarding consumers every day, you need to stand out from the crowd more than ever before. Think about how you can take your Unique Selling Proposition and turn it into your story.

Remember, the most important stories are not the ones you tell about your company or your product/service. It's the stories going on inside the heads of your customers and prospects that influence the decisions they make on a daily basis.

This is where you start to consider how you want to create your branded content. Your goal is to entertain and engage your audience, make them familiar with your brand, and keep them connected so they eventually become customers.

This is where emotional storytelling comes in. Can you illustrate how your brand can positively enhance the lives of your prospects in a story? To develop the relationship you want with consumers, your story needs to evoke the brand emotion of those relationships.

Think about captivating your readers by engrossing them in a story that offers a clear sense of progress and contrast from the "before" state to the "after" state. This is where your feature your organization's role in this transformation—after all, you are selling your organization's ability to make a difference.

In the water industry, we know that the health & well-being of children in a household is a hot button. We also know that photos of babies & children get high scores in terms of brand emotion. If your dealership has a tagline related to children, make sure you use the right photos to enhance your tagline; tell the story that goes with children, health and well-being.

Visual Impact - Remember the old saying "a picture is worth a thousand worlds"? In 2019, there is a huge emphasis on visual. Websites feature impactful "hero" photos on their landing pages. New space-saving icons are used to convey ideas more quickly than words and businesses continue to use photos to compel attention and interpret their message.

Core Message - Your story — your position — should weave throughout your messaging. What are the two or three words (or a brief concept) that you can continually use to bring your customer back to your Unique Selling Proposition / your story / the content you provide to create connections.

Omni-Channel Consistency - Is your branding consistent over multiple marketing channels? 2019 is all about omni-channel marketing.

Inspire Trust: Does your brand and stories inspire trust? In marketing, trust is everything. If they don't trust you, they won't buy from you. Think about it – every new customer represents a person whose trust has been earned. Every return customer represents a person whose trust continues to be held.

Updating a Well-Known Brand

New in 2018 – Culligan introduced its' new brand name, Culligan Water, to make younger consumers understand exactly what the company does. Looking to broaden and modernize its' appeal to millennial consumers, Culligan has dropped the word "man" from its' 60 year-old, well-recognized "Hey, Culligan Man" slogan. Even though this slogan has had a great run, the "man" part of it doesn't necessarily fit into today's environment and with today's younger consumers.

The new slogan, "Hey Culligan" will continue to resonate with consumers who remember the old slogan but the company feels it will also be relatable with its new target customer.

Changing any part of a well-established brand is scary. The company has rolled out a new series of ads featuring the different applications of Culligan treated water, from bathing to cooking to drinking, using a new company spokesperson, Cary Elwes, reprising his role from "The Princess Bride."

This new marketing campaign reflects Culligan's fresh direction and their strategy for tapping into the millennial generations' thirst for purified drinking water.

BTW – I have included an entire chapter on Marketing Water Filtration Products to Millennials. They are the future consumers of our industry.

Chapter 2.

The Basics

Wouldn't it be great if 5 people called your office everyday saying they needed a whole house system, they want it installed tomorrow and, by the way, they have the cash ready to pay for it right now.

Sure, it would be great but it's not realistic. That's why you need to get out there and market.

Facts:

Residential water treatment is an $18 billion industry. Drinking water alone makes up $2.5 billion of this annual revenue, with 42% of the population purchasing bottled water on a regular basis. Every day, we are bombarded with news about environmental spills, chemicals in our water, crumbling infrastructure.

Freedonia Group, a Cleveland-based research company, projects the U.S. consumer water treatment market to grow 4.4% a year to $1.6 billion by 2021, driven in part by a growing concern about drinking water quality.

Consumers know that they need to take the initiative to take care of their family's health and well-being.

You don't have to scare them, they're already scared enough. What you do need to do is let them know who you are, what your Dealership has to offer and why they should use you instead of your competition.

There are 2 main directions in Lead Generation marketing – Outbound and Inbound:

- Reaching out to find best prospects (Outbound)
- Creating the situations that allow prospects to find you (Inbound)

You need to have a presence in each.

Regardless of whether you are focusing on inbound or outbound marketing or which channel you select for your lead generation efforts, there are some basic marketing tenets that make a difference in your success.

- Defining your Top Prospects
- Developing Your Message
- Timing Your Marketing for Best Response
- Refining your Dealership's Marketing territory
- Generating Response with a Call to Action
- Testing Your Success

Chapter 3.

Defining Your Top Prospects

The key to a successful lead generation strategy – both Outbound and Inbound - is being able to identify who your best customers are and how to clone them.

Who are your best customers? Can you define them by their demographics, by their needs, by their life stage or lifestyle? Where are they?

Most of the experienced dealers I know can rattle off a customer profile the same way they can do their elevator pitch. Other dealers I work with tell me that they target "anyone interested in quality water".....which is code for "I really have no idea who to reach out to first."

Most Dealers tell me they want households with children who can pass credit. While this is a good place to start, there are a lot of other fish in the sea. If a dealership only focuses on one market segment, they're going to run out of prospects very quickly. But that segment is a great place to start.

Bottom line – thinking you know who your best clients are and actually knowing who they are may be two different things.

Since none of us have unlimited budgets for marketing & lead generation, we need to market smart. The entire rationale behind target marketing is no narrow the universe to the best possible market segments we can afford to reach.

Your goal is to focus your marketing dollars and brand message on the specific markets that are more likely to buy from you than other markets. This is a much more affordable, efficient, and effective way to reach potential clients and generate business.

With today's technology, a business can have their customer list analyzed at a very low cost and get a feel for their customers' basic demographics. An analysis can also tell you where your customers are.

These tools can be used to select look-alike prospects. In addition to the demographics (age, income, gender, marital status, ethnicity), there are analytic tools that can tell you about your customer's interests & activities (healthy lifestyle, golfer, gourmet cook, downhill skier, avid reader).

Real Life Example

Quality Drinking Water is in Broward County, FL. There are 725,000 households in Broward County, FL, of which 400,000 are home or condo owners. Quality Drinking cannot afford to direct mail to all 400,000 homeowners on a continuing basis nor afford what it costs in Pay Per Click advertising to come up 1st in Google Search. For Quality Drinking to generate an on-going flow of leads at a reasonable cost, they need to fine-tune this list of Broward County Homeowners by knowing who their best customers are and trying to cookie cutter them to create a workable prospect list to market.

By analyzing their own customer list, the owner of Quality Drinking was able to see that most of the systems they installed in Broward County in the last 2 years were to homes purchased in the past year were to Homeowners in single family homes with children.

There are 126,000 single family home owners with children in Broward County. We have now narrowed down the prospect universe to a much more manageable audience.

Based on the price of the system, a savvy dealer can further refine his or her prospect universe by overlaying home value, household income or a modeled credit score.

For this illustration, if we overlay a modeled credit score of 650 on top of the single family homeowners with children, our prospect audience narrows to 76,000 households.

Now, this is a number Quality Drinking Water can work with.

Creating a Persona

Some businesses rely on creating a Persona or Avatar that represents the common traits of their ideal customers. A customer Persona is a fictional customer, with a photo, name, and personality. A business can have more than one Persona. Many business owners use this device to describe their ideal customer in detail including what they wear, what their hobbies are and what concerns them. This helps them create a voice for their Persona which can be used to help shape the actual marketing message.

You can use the Persona you create to help tell your story.

For example, Cheryl Smith is the mother of 2 young children, age 2 and 4. She lives with her husband in a single family home in Richmond Virginia. Cheryl's husband Ron works for a Fortune 500 company and Cheryl herself works part-time while the kids are at school. Their friends /cohorts typically have children as well and Cheryl plans play dates at local parks and at the homes of friends.

Cheryl is active and in good shape; she is very concerned about her family's health & well-being. She is interested in healthy cooking, the environment and home décor.

You can use a simple worksheet like this to help you develop a basic Persona. There are lots of other models available, simple Google Persona templates....but this gives you a place to start.

Persona Profile for: "BUSY MOM"

Age Range: _____

Key Responsibilities: _____

Major Concerns: _____

Key Stressors/Pain Points: _____

Key Purchase Drivers: _____

Place(s) Most Likely to Find Information_____

Preferred Content Medium: _____

Days/Times Most Likely to Consume Content:_____

Role in Purchase Process for Family: _____

Look at the landing page of the RainSoft website. It must have been designed for Cheryl's persona. The site highlights a series of photos that tell the RainSoft story while speaking to

Cheryl as a mother, featuring pictures of a cute little girl and a mom washing her son's hands under the faucet with the tag line "fix my water", an environmental mood shot titled "reduce your ecological footprint", a shot of Cheryl and her husband rinsing lettuce leaves together "healthier water for your home".

Cheryl may be one of several Personas you develop to help define your Dealership's best prospects.

> **TIP:**
>
> *Developing your Dealership's target personas is a great exercise you can carry out with your team.*

Using Outside Lists to Find Your Dealership's Best Prospects

Lists can be developed for direct mail, telemarketing, emailing and social media marketing. While you have many choice is terms of the marketing channel you are planning to use, the bottom line is that you need to pick the right people for your product.

You don't need a crystal ball for this. Remember, not everyone is your prospect. If you are selling high priced whole house systems, you certainly don't want to waste your precious advertising dollars promoting your product to renters.

While many printers espouse Every Door Direct Mail, EDDM is not for you. You need to spend your money efficiently and use todays' technology to slice and dice the available universe and pick your best shots.

There are literally thousands of mailing lists – In a broad sense, we categorize them as

- Hotline Lists
- Compiled Lists
- Lifestyle Lists
- Response Lists
- Modeled Lists

Hotline Lists

Hotline Lists are also referred to as Trigger lists – in other words, a household's presence on a Hotline list is triggered by something....and, at the same time, we anticipate that their presence on the list will trigger a buying decision.

Hotline files include New Homeowners, New Movers, Parents of New Babies, New Mortgages, New Businesses, New Phone connects, New Magazine subscribers, New Divorces, Newly Engaged, College Graduates, Individuals Turning 65, Parents of Children Turning 1, Individuals Turning 50.

> *TIP:*
>
> *In the Water Industry, the New Homeowner and New Parents lists are the top lists. According to the 2017 WQA Consumer Opinion Study, over 60% of new homeowners purchased systems in the first year they are in their new home.*

The most important list in the Hotline list category is the New Homeowner List. One of the reasons that this list is so effective is that the water never tastes the same in the new home and in the old home. Year-after-year, The New Homeowner lists remain the #1 prospect list in the Water Quality Industry.

Compiled lists

These lists are sourced from many different places and aggregated into a large database. Information is pulled from various sources to add depth to a given household record and allow a marketer to hone in on their best prospects.

There are many sources in the marketplace for age, gender and household composition. Other demographics, such as swimming pool ownership may be sourced from Property files, ethnicity from models created by Ethnic Technologies, mortgage information from courthouse records, children's age information from new birth records, and so on.

Every large compiler has their own "rules" for adding records into their database and maintaining their files. They are not all the same. Make sure you ask all the right questions, including when the last time the list was updated.

For Water Quality Dealers, the current top responders in the Compiled List category is Families with Children...but all eyes are on Millennials who will be the next big group of water quality products buyers.

> **TIP:**
>
> *According to the WQA Consumer Study, 32% of water system purchases were made by Families with Children. What dealer would not want to target this key market group?*

Lifestyle Lists

These households have a propensity for certain lifestyle activities. Once again, this type of information is compiled from websites, magazine subscriptions, contest entries or surveys. Examples include active skiers, golfers, gamblers, cruisers, health enthusiasts, pet owners, gourmet cooks, outdoor aficionados, healthy living, gardening, football fans, NASCAR fanatics, video gamers, sweepstakes/lottery participants.

TIP:

The 2017 WQA Consumer Study found that 69% of consumers who bought a system stated that their desire for a healthy lifestyle was the reason they bought a water filtration system.

The entire question of Health and healthy lifestyle is most visible in the baby boomer group. The boomer mantra is "if you have your health". As boomers age, they continue to see how being healthy impacts every phase of their lives. Boomers still have the most disposable income of any market segment. A dealership that wants to increase business today needs to focus their energy on health conscious boomers.

Response Lists

These households have self-reported that they have a particular interest, engage in a specific activity, have a particular ailment, enjoy a genre of music, subscribe to a particular magazine, donate to charitable organizations.

This information may be compiled from websites, subscriptions or surveys. Additionally, mailing list compilers have agreements with different organizations to trade data or enhance their own data using other company's information.

TIP:

For Water Dealers, Ailment Sufferers may be a great niche. Soft water is a necessity for individuals with psoriasis and eczema. In terms of other ailment sufferers, CDC studies show that individuals with ailments are highly susceptible to water-borne bacteria.

Modeled lists

Sometimes, in cases where we do not have specifically sourced information, models have been created to pinpoint households using generalities.

You've heard of the expression "birds of a feather flock together"? List companies look at lots of variables to create these models. For example, a list company can take a list of households who are known to be regular international cruisers. The analysts look at the other variables in those households and then cookie-cutter those variables on "unknown" households, thereby modeling a list of households for their propensity to cruise.

Modeled data works in many ways. Typically, models are done in deciles (10% segments) and marketers can choose to select the top model within the model.

In the Water Quality arena, many dealerships use Modeled Credit Data to locate prospects who can afford to buy their systems.

There are great companies in the marketplace that specialize in providing high quality direct mail lists. There are also some not-so-great ones. One caveat – if the price seems too good to be true, question the list.

TIP: Looking for Free Market research?

The WQA publishes a Consumer opinion Study every few years. Every Dealer needs to read this Study. The information provided by this Study is worth the price of membership.

If you want to find out more about the people in your market, go on-line to the US Government Census and find out about your specific market.

Ask your list company for free counts in your market (everyone will give you free counts).

Chapter 4.

Developing Your Message

Regardless of whether you are using an Inbound or Outbound strategy, when it comes to lead generation, businesses need to ask themselves if their product is a NEED or a WANT.

Consumers spend their money on things they absolutely NEED first. Then, they spend their disposable dollars on things they WANT.

Examples:

- New Homeowners WANT their homes to look nice when company arrives. But in their area, they NEED a system to take the iron out of the water to avoid unsightly rust stains on their sidewalks.

- Parents of new babies WANT their children to be healthy. They NEED a system to insure that the water they are offering their children is safe and secure.
- Millennials WANT to live social, socially acceptable lives. They NEED a system because there is no way they would ever serve tap water at a dinner party.
- Dog Owners WANT their pets to livelong lives. They NEED a system to insure their dogs are drinking the best water for their health.
- Ailment sufferers WANT to feel better. They NEED quality water to down their medications.

It's much easier to sell a NEED than a want...and it's your job to position the quality water options you provide in such a way that a want becomes a need.

The top copywriters suggest that asking questions is the best way to involve the reader, whether it is in print copy, envelope teaser or email subject line.

Remember, when it comes to lead generation, your job is to lead that horse to water. If the written word is not your thing, look towards hiring an agency or a copywriter to actually write the verbiage. There are very talented people out there who can really convince consumers that their lives will become a shamble if they don't have a water conditioner.

Here are some examples of using leading questions to involve the reader and move the conversation from a want into a NEED.

Examples:

- Do you ever get that chlorine smell from your tap water? You NEED a proper Water filter to get your water quality up-to-sniff.
- Do your sidewalks have rust stains? You NEED a water system that will remove calcium and lime and give your home the curb appeal you can be proud of.
- Do your white clothes look dingy when they come out of the wash? You NEED an eco-friendly laundry system that make your whites sparkle and saves you money
- Do you enjoy entertaining in your home? You NEED a water filtration system so you can serve your guests quality filtered water.

Remember Cheryl from the previous chapter? This is where using a Persona like Cheryl might be a great tool for a business when they are trying to convert a want to a NEED.

A Water Quality Dealer could market to Cheryl and her cohorts (Homeowners with Children) with a message of health & well-being for her children and family, highlighting the virtues of quality water for health, whether it be for drinking, cooking or bathing. For Cheryl and her family, pure water is not a want but a real NEED.

TIP:

Use Action Words to Create an Engaging Message:

We know that specific words are actionable and marketers can increase their response rates simply by changing a word or two.

Marketing guru Pat Freisen explains that certain dynamic verbs are so powerful that it doesn't matter whether it is a subject line of an e-mail, teaser copy on an envelope, the headline of a post or even a tweet – the right verb can make a dramatic difference in the response or open rate.

This is the list of the top 54 Verbs that Help Convert prospects into customers:

act	learn
add	make
apply	master
boost	pack
buy	plan
build	perfect
call	polish
choose	read
claim	receive
click	reduce

compare	register
confirm	reply
connect	save
contact	see
discover	send
download	share
explore	shop
find	sign (up)
follow	start
get	take
grab	talk
go	try
improve	tweet
increase	update
join	view
kickstart	visit
keep	watch

As always, marketers need to test to see which one performs best for their individual direct marketing program.

I do get it - it's not easy to create direct mail copy that works. We can learn by testing or we can simply go with what works.

TIP:

Trim your copy to make it more effective:

- *Know your objective and have a clear call to action for the reader (e.g. Call 1-800-XXX-XXXX today...or Order today for your Free Gift).*

- *Always include a P.S. Many people read the P.S. first, so don't waste it. It always lifts response.*

- *Create a sense of urgency.*

- *Read your copy out loud and get rid of all the extra words ~~that~~ you don't use when you talk. "That" is the most overused word – it can almost always be eliminated.*

- *It's OK to start a sentence with "and" or "but."*

- *Keep sentences short.*

- *Use bullets with active words. We've all learned to skim. Make it easy for your reader to read & understand your message and act on it quickly*

Chapter 5.

Timing Your Marketing for Best Response The Art of Syncographics

Syncographics - This is more commonly referred to as Market Timing.

While traditional direct marketing response has been characterized as 40% list – 40% offer – and 20% creative, the new way of thinking includes another piece into the puzzle which addresses market timing – what I like to call Syncographics.

The truth is that syncographics significantly affects response.

There are specific life stages that force buying – moving, buying a home, having a baby, getting married, getting divorced, graduating college, Turning 65, getting a new job.

I want to circle back to the 2 top life stage events that trigger the purchase of a water filtration unit: the purchase of a home and the birth of a baby. When it comes to generating leads, these life stage events are easy lists to obtain. Dealers can either buy them from a list company or get them from local newspapers or courthouses.

Regardless of where you obtain this data, these are top-top prospects for your Dealership. You need to reach out to them at the right time – meaning in the first year they are in the new home or in the first year they have that new baby, and make sure you refer to their special

Special Events:

You might also want to consider how you can market within the framework of the traditional holidays like Christmas, Mother's Day, Father's Day, Halloween and what I call the Hallmark list of holidays: Bosses Day, Teacher's Day, Secretary's Day and my most recent favorite – Grandparents Day.

There are also special days that Water dealerships can use to create interest, whether it be for direct mail or creating content for direct mail, press releases, Facebook posts and tweets:

- World Water Day (March 22, 2019)

- National Drinking Water Week (May 5-11, 2019)
- National Coffee Day (September 29, 2019)

Mother Nature also gets into the act. Hurricanes, flooding, hail storms, and environmental spills all create "need to buy" situations that marketers can actually plan for.

Factoring syncographics into our marketing mix gives us a lift in response; forgetting about market timing will ruin a perfectly good campaign.

It pays to be prepared

In the past few years we have learned that water contamination reports and boil water alerts are more common than we'd like to see. Dealers need to look at this as a marketing opportunity.

I know water dealers who keep postcards on hand for boil water alerts in their area. By reacting quickly, they assume the mantle of expert - It always pays to be prepared. Let's refer back to the WQA Consumer Opinion Study. 89% of consumers bought some kind of water filter after a boil water alert – 12% of them buying RO units.

Unfortunately, the occurrence of a disaster, whether courtesy of Mother Nature or an environmental spill, is not a question of *if*, it's just a question of *when*.

TIP:

Keep bottles of water on hand, labeled with your Dealership's contact information to distribute at shelters, give away when an emergency arises. This is great community service and terrific PR for your Dealership.

In recent years, Culligan International and Culligan Dealers have provided bottled water through Convoy of Hope to the victims of Hurricane Sandy and the devastating tornadoes in Oklahoma as part of the CulliganCares program.

BTW - This is the also kind of initiative that resonates with the Millennial generation.

Chapter 6.

Refining Your Dealership's Marketing Territory

No Water Dealer should spend one cent on advertising outside of their territory. After all, why spend good money marketing water filtration units for another dealership?

With any form of direct marketing, be it direct mail, telemarketing, email, Facebook or door-to-door – Dealers can be very specific in their geographic pull.

Options include selections by zip-code or county, radius mileage, drive time or even creating a specific map of a given area.

This ability to finely tune territory is what separates direct marketing from print, radio/TV, magazine or shared mail advertising.

That is what makes direct marketing cost-effective and efficient.

Chapter 7.

Generating Response with Your Offer

Every direct marketing effort must contain a call to action, which is defined as a piece of content intended to induce a viewer, reader, or listener to perform a specific act, typically taking the form of an instruction or directive (e.g. *buy now, click here, fill out this form today*).

So you need to make a proper inducement. We call that **The Offer.**

People aren't stupid. They can see straight through a lukewarm offer. When consumers think you're trying to put something over on them, you lose everything you accomplished with your great list selection, copy & design.

Bottom line - if you aren't making a worthy offer – forget it.

The offer can also become part of the theme of your communication. In many industries, I often see the offer being tacked on as kind of an "Oops – I almost forgot it" kind of thing. Begin with it. Restate it. Denote its key benefits. Create the actual copy around it so it's incorporated into the entire program.

Depending on the nature of the communication and what you want to accomplish, there are different kinds of direct marketing offers:

- **Lead generation offers**

  Lead generation offers are typically free offers designed to get someone to raise their hands and say "I'm interested!" (and give us their info so we can connect with them) In the Water Quality Industry, common lead generation offers include gifts like family-sized tide, diapers, soaps, coupon books, gift cards to home improvement stores.

- **Order generation offers**

  Order generation offers are paid offers. "Buy Now / Pay Later", "No interest until 2018". When people respond to these offers, they are committing to pay at a later date. This is common in the Furniture Industry, there are offers like we will deliver your new sofa now / pay in 6 months. And, yes, it is also common in the water quality industry.

- **Continuity offers**

  Continuity offers are for companies that sell products on a monthly basis. "Try us before you commit". The offers used for these types of companies are usually free trials for a specific period followed by an agreed-upon monthly billing. In the Water Industry, "Try our salt delivery service for one month – and if you like it, sign up for our convenient monthly service".

- **Traffic building offers**

  Traffic building offers are most often used by retailers who want to see their stores packed with customers. The most common traffic building offers are discount coupons, BOGOs, Gift with Purchase or free event promotions. In the Water Industry, these are mostly used by the "big box" stores like Home Depot, Lowes or Sears.

Three more things:

1. The offer is an implied contract between you and your prospect so you need to be clear in what you're committing to. "Buy 1 Get 1 free" can also mean "Buy 100 Get 100 free". Can you afford that? Make sure you really understand what you're offering.

2. Keep in mind what I said about lukewarm offers. I remember when dentists thought they could offer "free

bitewing x-rays" – like that was something a person just couldn't wait for. And they wondered why their response dropped like a rock. The savvy dental marketer is offering a free whitening session, which is an offer that people actually want.

3. To be successful in any direct response campaign, you need to use the right response vehicle. When you make it easy for people to respond in the way they prefer, you get more responses.

Here are the Top 7 Direct Response Mechanisms for 2019

1. Phone — Provide a phone number for people to call. If you are able, use a special number to track your responses, if not, give them a response code that they will need to provide when they call in.

2. Personalized QR Codes – you can create special QR codes for each campaign to help drive responders to a special landing page on your website....Take a look at our latest personalized QR Code and let me know what you think!

3. Website — Create a special landing page just for the campaign. You can track who has looked at it, as well as who actually filled out the form.

4. Mail – BREs still work for certain offers.

5. Email — Provide an email address that they can respond to and not something generic like "office@". Use a real name for best results. People still want to communicate with people.

6. Text — Allow people to text to respond by providing a text short code.

7. Come In — If you have a brick & mortar location, give people the option to come in and see you. Make sure you provide a street address and google map icon for their convenience.

Needless to say, when you are calculating your bottom line results, the key is testing to see which one works best for your particular campaign.

TIP:

In the Water Quality Industry, Free In-Home Water Testing as a standalone offer doesn't make the phone ring. The Water Test is a means to the sale....but offering it is not what will generate the actual lead.

Chapter 8.

Testing Your Success

One of the real benefits of direct marketing is that you can tell if your marketing campaign worked. This goes for and of our direct marketing channels, including direct mail, telemarketing and digital marketing.

You can even test different elements of a campaign by inserting key-codes on the response mechanism, utilizing different 800 call-in numbers, or even by directing responders to unique different landing pages.

You can also use Google Analytics to help you determine where your traffic, and therefore, response is coming from.

How to Compute Response

Customers are always asking me what percent response they can expect from a direct mail campaign. I always explain that response is based on the list, the creative, the offer and market timing – all important factors that go hand-in-hand to determine response.

But when they want to know how to actually figure it out, there's an easy approach to determining a response. Let's use a direct mail campaign for this example:

- Project the cost of your direct mail program. Since I'm no math wiz, let's keep it simple by assuming the budget is $1,000 on the mailing list, printing, addressing, postage, etc.

- Calculate the profit you will clear, on average, with every response. Again, for simplicity's sake, let's say that each response will bring you $100 in net revenue.

- Therefore – You need only 10 responses to break even (10 responses x $100 = $1,000). So with a mailing to 1,000 people, just 1 percent would be a good response. If the mailing was to 2,000 people (with same $1,000 cost), just one-half of 1 percent would be good. If you mailed to 2,000 people and each respondent made two purchases, then a mere response of one-quarter of 1 percent would be good.

But all percentages aside, bottom line – if they made more $$ then they spent the first time they did a mailing, they can consider it a successful program. They gained customers – whose value will increase as they stay customers (lifetime value), they brought new leads into the business that they may close at a later date, and they learned from the experience, allowing them to tweak future mailings for even greater success.

You can use the same approach to testing for any outbound channel.

> **TIP:**
>
> *Consider using different QR (Quick Response) codes on your direct mailers, segmented by market, to drive consumers to different landing pages. You can easily track whether this is working.*

Chapter 9.

Deciding On Your Marketing Channels

Regardless of whether you are focusing on Outbound or Inbound Lead Generation, the core direct marketing principles (marketing to the right audience, having solid creative, making a good offer and timing it right) still apply.

In 2017, we focused on developing an integrated approach to reach out to people through a combination of marketing channels, using the same message and offer and timing the campaign arrival to insure that the message gets in home at the same time for best response. There is an entire chapter on Multi-Channel Marketing coming up.

In 2018, we are still advocating outreach through multiple channels, but the Engagement Marketing philosophy hinges on our being able to *move* the prospect from one marketing channel to another.

With Engagement Marketing, the game plan is to increase the amount of time customers spend looking at your material through the marketing channels, researching your company, becoming fans, learning to trust you.

Use direct mail, email, social media and even telemarketing, where it's appropriate, for your outreach. Try to move your audience from one marketing channel to another to increase their engagement. The more time people spend moving from channel to channel, the better your chances of converting them.

Here's the scenario. You send out a direct mail campaign. The mailer includes a QR Code that can be scanned so that the recipient is directed to your website. She visits your website and sees an interesting YouTube video and watches it. At the end of the video, she can be directed back to another part of your website.

She has no more time and decides to log off. When she exits your site, a pop up appears, asking for her email address and phone #, offering a quick download of recipes. Between the mail, website and You tube video, she has spent a decent amount of time visiting with you and she has a comfort level with your company. Chances are good that she will complete your lead generation form so you can move her along the sales funnel.

That's what you want to happen.

Every business owner needs to test a variety of marketing channels and develop the most responsive sequence to use to move the customer through the funnel.

Technology continues to change and the marketing landscape broadens every year with new options added into the mix.

In the following chapters, we will be looking at the key lead generation marketing channels in the Water Quality Industry:

- Direct Mail
- Email Marketing
- Telemarketing
- Display Ads / sponsored posts on Facebook & Instagram
- Online Lead Generation
- Search Engine Marketing
- Social Media – Blogging, Facebook, Linked In, Twitter
- Trade Shows
- Door-to-Door
- Putting it all together with an Integrated Multi-Channel Approach

TIP:

Are you making sure your posts and press releases are getting published? There are lots of online resources that help you increase the visibility of your brand:

Check out Feedspot - https://www.feedspot.com/

You might also want to look at the different Press Release distribution companies, like PRWire , PR Newswire or PR.com.

Ask your local Chamber of Commerce if they post member blogs..

That would also be a valuable backlink from an SEO perspective.

Chapter 10.

Direct Mail – It's Back with a Vengeance

The granddaddy of lead generation, Direct Mail still generates leads efficiently and cost-effectively.

It is the *only* medium guaranteed to get right into the home of your best prospects. It is dependable and gives you an opportunity to state your case in a compelling way – using text, photos, and the right call to action.

It's easy to rent a quality direct mail list, finely targeted to your best possible prospects. You don't have to worry about anyone blocking your message - the USPS will reliably deliver your mailer. As far as the creative piece, nowadays you can go on-line and find lots of templates you can use & adapt to create an attractive mail piece.

Just like in any direct marketing campaign, the 4 key factors in Direct Mail Response: List, Creative, Offer and Market Timing. And, of course, each element needs to be tested & tweaked for success.

Creating a Mail Piece

A good direct mailer combines both the look of the mail piece and the marketing copy. There are many agencies in the marketplace that specialize in direct response creative and they will sit down with you, review your product, goals and budget and help to create the campaign you want.

Many small businesses will do this themselves, adapting mailers that they get from their home office or receive in the mail from their competitors.

Speaking of adaptation - here's a very cool idea borrowed from the Food & Beverage Industry. To generate excitement around a new water-enhancing product, one company created a magazine ad with hydrochromic ink. When you looked at the ad, the all-white page featured a full glass of water with text that prompted consumers to cover the page in water.

When the page got wet, the print ad revealed a secret message highlighting this thrilling application of water and made sure to remind readers that the new product could make a "boring drink" awesome again. What a great idea.

> **TIP:**
>
> *This concept is easily adaptable to a direct mail postcard. Can you imagine getting a postcard in the mail that says "pour water on me". Like magic, the hidden message appears, extoling the virtues of quality water, complete with your tagline and offer. This is the kind of creative direct mail marketing that stands out and wows consumers. Talk about really making an impression.*

Other tips for 2019 include shaped mailers that stand out in the mail box or bumpy mailers that beg to be opened. You want your mail piece to be conspicuous; you want it to shine. Use bright colors, textured paper, and memorable fonts.

For those businesses owners who want to experiment with doing this on their own – here's a quick tip. Go to Fiverr.com. This is a website where you can engage an individual to provide you with the marketing services you need for your project, including graphic & design services, writing & translation, video & animation and online marketing….and all for the whopping cost of $5.00. This is probably the largest virtual staffing agency in the world. I have used Fivver resources to create a Facebook banner, update my logo and change the background on some artwork for my website. It's a site you should seriously check out.

Incorporating Digital as a Companion

Marketers can take advantage of Informed Delivery, a benefit from the United States Postal Service. This program gives consumers who sign up a daily digital preview of their physical mail and boasts a 67% open rate.

Every morning, I get an email from the U.S.P.S. that shows me the mail I can expect to receive in my mailbox that day. I have a chance to take a look to see what's coming in, and for some offers, actually click on a live link that brings me to a catalog or website.

From a consumer perspective, this is a great example of an omni-channel marketing experience since the customer gets the same message in multiple marketing channels.

From a business marketing perspective, this offers your Dealership a chance to have your marketing message seen twice – once in print and once on line – for the same postage cost. This gives your direct mail extra "legs", and an additional opportunity for engagement which increases response.

To give you an understanding about how this actually works, when a direct mailing is ready to go, the mailing and the mailing list itself are brought to the representative at the Post Office. The mailing list is then matched against the Informed Delivery subscribers. As of January 1, 2019, there are over 16 million consumers opted-in to Informed Delivery.

The mailing list can be your existing customers or a prospect list of homeowners you buy from a mailing list provider. When the actual mailers are sent through the mail, the consumers on your mailing list who are signed up for the service, get a digital copy of your mailer in their in box.

As I mentioned before, Informed Delivery also provides companies with the ability to do an image replacement, so instead of showing a black-and-white image of what's coming in the mail, they can incorporate color and graphics and even a link to their catalog or website. This gives companies a way to get their marketing message front and center.

By the way, the U.S. Postal Service is a great resource for new direct mail marketing ideas. They also offer lots of case studies and examples on their site. Click here.

Chapter 11.

Email Marketing

I could write an entire book about Email Marketing; when it works, when it doesn't work.

So many businesses felt that email marketing was going to be the panacea of marketing. Everyone hoped email marketing would be low cost and effective. We could email to everyone and people would be thrilled to get our email messages. But that didn't happen.

Think about your own email in-box. How many email messages do you get each day? Do they all go into your in-box or do some filter into your spam or delete folder? Do you read them all? Scan the subject lines? Do you open everything?

Are you comfortable opening anything that comes from an unknown sender?

The truth is that a percentage of email messages are trashed by either the recipient – or by the ISP (internet service provider) who acts as your personal gatekeeper, sometimes whether you want them to or not.

Making Email Marketing Work

In successful email marketing, quantity and frequency are the real drivers. People need to get used to seeing your name and that comes with frequency. A single email deployment isn't going to generate dozens of leads. You need to look at email marketing as part of a program; a series of well-planned communications designed to get your name out to your prospects so that they know who you are and will click on your message.

Businesses that use email as a marketing tool in conjunction with other marketing channels will also get a lift in response. While we know that frequency has a tremendous impact on response, it's not just about how many times a message is received by a prospect, it's also about the number of ways that message is received.

In addition to using Informed Delivery, many businesses are partnering email with direct mail, now that email appending processes have gotten less expensive to do. They are timing their campaigns so that both the mail and the email are delivered the same day.

Remember, in 2019, we are focusing on omni-channel marketing engagement. Regardless of the marketing channel, it's important to present a similar look and feel to your material and offer comparable messaging. That will boost brand recognition and up the response for each marketing channel.

There is no question that email can work for you – as long as you have reasonable expectations about the response you imagine you'll get.

Developing an Email List

The best email lists are self-generated. That means your goal is to collect email addresses from your customers, fans & prospects so you can keep in touch with them electronically.

Did you know that your email list naturally degrades by approximately 22.5% every year? That's why it is so important to continuously grow your email list and make up for these lost subscribers.

Here are a few ways you can grow your e-mail list:

- Collect email addresses at Home Shows, community fairs.

- Offer a great lead magnet to encourage visitors to share their email address. A lead magnet can be a giveaway item, a pocket flashlight, water test, recipe cards.

- Host a giveaway. Require participants to sign up with their email address, and give them additional entries when they share the giveaway on social media.

- Host a photo contest for World Water Week with a prize for the best photo.

- Create a quiz and require that participants enter their email address before they can download their results. There are on-line tools to do this.

- Offer a coupon in exchange for an email address if you have an eCommerce site.

- Make some of your content gated. Gated content is content on your website that can't be accessed until the visitor enters their email address

- Add sharing buttons to your email signature, your thank you page, and to your lead magnets themselves so that your existing subscribers can spread the word for you.

- Add a sign up button to your Facebook Page.

- Add a call to action to your website About page with an inline opt-in form.
- Speak at the local Church, PTA or Chamber of Commerce and collect email addresses.
- Use paid search ads to drive qualified traffic to your opt-in landing page.
- Add a QR code to all your printed materials and link it to your opt-in landing page.
- Add a fishbowl to your counter (if people walk into your dealership) with a chance to win a prize.
- Keep your opt-in form simple: you should only ask for first name and email maximum. Only ask for an email address if you can.
- Add a call to action to your Facebook cover photo, encouraging visitors to sign up with their email.
- Post a sign outside your Dealership that encourages passers-by to sign up for your email list.
- Ask your existing subscribers to forward your emails to a friend by including a "Forward to a Friend" button at the bottom of your newsletters or emails
- Start a loyalty program to encourage your customers to sign up for your email list.
- Start a birthday club to reward those who sign-up for your email list with special discounts and bonuses on their birthday.

- Reward subscribers or employees for referring their friends to join.
- Offer different lead magnets for different segments of your audience. For example, a container of Tide for a Family with Children, a fancy water-bottle for a millennial female.

- One-up the competition with your lead magnet by making it bigger and better. For example, if your competition is offering a 30-point checklist, make yours a 50-point checklist.
- Publicize your anti-spam policy right below the submit button on your opt-in form to increase conversions. For example, *"Your email address is 100% secure and we will never sell your information to a 3rd party."*

TIP:

Consider using a Lead Magnet to collect email data. Consider the right incentive you can give away for free to entice people to share their email address with you.

Buying an Email List

If I had a dollar for every time a client asked to buy an email list, I could retire today! I want to divide my comments into 2 parts – buying a standalone email list versus appending email data to your direct mail list.

Email, as a standalone marketing channel, produces marginal response and can negatively impact your business. Most marketing experts recommend against it. However, day after day, we still get requests to buy an email list.

There are many email lists in the marketplace that are for sale – some are ok, some are totally not. E-mail addresses tend to change frequently, which makes keeping a list clean a real challenge. There also may be multiple email addresses at a given household, including household members of all ages.

Unfortunately, many of the people who sell email lists make a lot of false claims about the list ("this list is so good you'll get a 5% response"). You may find that these lists are missing data, contain out-of-date information or have been illegally harvested, which is a violation of the CAN-SPAM Act.

Bottom line, while it might sound great to get an email list with 5,000 or 10,000 names overnight, it's going to be pretty worthless if it's an out-of-date list full of inaccurate data.

But, if you are still determined to buy an email list, make sure you insist that the email addresses be verified and only pay for those email addresses that have been verified as deliverable.

The email verification processes that are available in the marketplace can eliminate the invalid email addresses so you are not sending to phantom addresses. While this may not enhance the list quality, it will certainly impact the final quantity and the list cost.

Last, while you may think that you can buy an email list and load it into your Constant Contact, Mail Chimp or basic e-mail broadcast software, this is seriously frowned upon by all the contact management providers in the marketplace. If they find you have been broadcasting to rented or pirated lists, they will shut your account down faster than you can say spam.

For those companies who are focused on email marketing, there are more robust (and more expensive) platforms that will allow you to ebroadcast.

Email Appending

When you append emails to a direct mail list, you get the chance to "double dip" your message and get another touchpoint at a very low cost. Remember, 2019 is the year of omni-channel marketing. You want your prospect to see your message in more than one channel. This enhances your branding efforts and makes your message more important.

An email appending service takes the list you provide and matches it against a multi-sourced, email driven consumer database. Be sure you ask your service provider to use a CAN-SPAM compliant list.

There are different match options – individual, household and address. The match I would recommend depends on what you're offering. The tighter the match, the smaller the quantity matched. In the water treatment industry, you might decide that any household in a given market is a prospect and opt for the broadest match. If you were in financial services, you would want to match on an individual level.

Typically, e-mail addresses can be located for 15% – 25% of a Consumer list.

Bottom line, keeping an e-mail list pristine is challenging and expensive to maintain. For many marketers, it's totally worth the effort.

> **TIP:**
>
> *Update your entire email database at least once a year. Many businesses do this by emailing a Holiday Card to their lists. Once you see which addresses bounced, you can correct or delete. This will also give people an opportunity to unsubscribe.*

Retargeting

This is a great way to maximize the investment you've made to collect and append email addresses and communicate your message in yet another marketing channel.

Email retargeting lets you supplement your email marketing campaign with display advertising. With retargeting, you can serve ads to people who open your emails as well as people who don't. All you need is an email address. They don't have to visit your website, click on, or even open an email. You can serve retargeted display ads to each and every person on your email list.

This technique is an incredibly powerful tool for marketers who want to reach out and keep their brand in front of their email list without sending more emails and risking mass unsubscribes.

Email retargeting is extremely effective at building multiple touch points with customers and keeping your brand front and forward. When used in conjunction with an email or direct mail campaign, it can drastically improve the reach of your marketing program.

E-mail Deployments

There are lots of good e-mail providers in the marketplace who will provide the list and do the deployment on your behalf. You can work with a "white-listed" e-mail provider to get your message into your prospects' in-boxes. The term

white-listed means that the ISPs will let e-mail broadcasts from that company go through their systems. These companies have a good reputation with the ISPs. They cherish and cultivate their white-listed status. In most cases, a white-listed provided will not even take your personal e-mail list to add to the deployment because they don't know how you compiled & updated your data and they cannot take the chance that the list will bounce.

On the negative side, using an outside company to do frequent deployments can become a very expensive proposition since you have to pay for each ebroadcast.

Using Email for CRM

Email is the top marketing channel CRM (customer relationship management). If someone knows you and trusts you, they will open your e-mail. If they don't know you, the chances of getting that email opened and read are slim.

For Dealerships who want to stay in touch with their customers, send out reminders, product updates and generally stay in touch, e-mail is a fabulous tool.

Standing Out from the Crowd

The same way it's important for a mail piece to stand out in the mail box, your email message needs to be memorable to be opened, Subject line and teaser copy are important. You need to pique your prospect's interest. Remember, their inbox has been flooded with emails from lots of companies vying for their attention. You need to be noticed.

Much has been written about subject lines. Best practices suggest that the subject line be no more than 50 characters – you want the subject line to be readable in its entirety. How do you pique someone's interest? Should your subject line tease, should it tempt – should it be straightforward?

Since your first impression will be your subject line, here are a few best- practice tips to help you break through the clutter.

Create compelling subject lines

- Keep it short so it fully displays in the reader's browser window (under 50 characters)
- Start with the most important words

- Be specific
- Use numbers
- Convey a sense of Urgency. *"Act now", "limited time"*
- Ask questions – This engages your readers and will encourage them to open your email to find out the answer.
- Use the preview line (sometimes called a pre-header, sometimes called a teaser line). This displays right after the subject line when your reader views the email in the inbox. It helps get the reader's attention
- Testing - consider dividing your email broadcast into 2 groups using different subject lines and seeing which performs better.

E-mail marketing, just like any other form of direct marketing, needs to be tested and tweaked. You will need to test your subject line, list and offer – until you hit the magic combination that generates Leads day-in, day-out.

> **TIP:**
>
> *Convey a sense of Urgency. Use phrases like "Act now", "limited time", "Don't delay"*

Chapter 12.

Telemarketing

Poor Telemarketing. Because of the Do Not Call, what was once a thriving & highly profitable source of consumer lead generation has taken a back seat to other marketing channels.

Don't get me wrong, in the Consumer World, telemarketing is still terrific for appointment setting, confirmation, follow up, customer relationship management (CRM).....but for down and dirty lead generation, it's just the way it was in the old days – when it delivered great leads at a low cost.

Nowadays, most households are either listed on the Do Not Call or have become "untethered". Untethered is the word we use to describe someone who no longer is tethered to a landline and uses their mobile phone for all of their communications.

For Dealers that want to append cell phone #s to their customer lists, it has become a simple, inexpensive process. Many Dealers are using cell phone contact to update their customers.

I do want to make a couple of quick comments on Residential Telemarketing.

Some companies/organizations are exempt from the Do Not Call laws. They may be non-profits, market research firms, or political fundraisers (amazing how they got exempt from the law, isn't it). Of course that has not stopped the flow of telemarketing calls from offshore companies, robocalls or businesses who just don't care. If you're like me, you still receive several unsolicited calls a day. While I rarely get testy with the telemarketer on the phone, there are people out there who gleefully report those businesses who call them to either their state watchdog or to the FTC.

There are other companies who suggest that there are exemptions in terms of when someone gets on a list and when the DNC applies to them. All I can tell you is have your lawyer read the material on the DNC site and counsel you accordingly.

Be smart. Follow the rules. While you may feel that your company is doing market research, the FTC might not see it the same way.

Water Dealerships Succeed by Reaching Businesses by Phone

Businesses have always big users of coolers and bottled water. In today's eco-sensitive environment, many businesses are installing systems to provide their employees with quality water refill station that they can use to refill the bottles they bring from home. We also see these in airports, malls and other public places. This is another growth area for Water Filtration Dealers.

On Curb Your Enthusiasm, Susie said "who serves tap water at a dinner party?" Well I say "who serves tap water at a good restaurant?"

I'm not alone. I have seen people actually walk out of a restaurant out of principle. OK, I live in Boca Raton.

For Water Quality Dealers, restaurants should be low-hanging fruit.

Business marketing lists are fairly inexpensive. You can reach them through telemarketing during the day and actually set up appointments for a daytime visit. Email addresses can be appended to the list, giving dealers another marketing channel to use. Plus, when the rep is at a restaurant for an appointment, it's a piece of cake to visit neighboring restaurants at the same time.

As an offer - you can provide personalized glass bottles for their servers to pour then leave on the table. Customers really appreciate this. For the restaurant, this is great customer service and a personalized bottle is a wonderful branding tool.

Restaurants are not the only big users of quality water.

Doctor offices and clinics must have filtered water to offer to their patients. Yes, these types of businesses are currently water cooler customers but the people who work at these offices know the value of quality water and are great prospects. In the old days, when telephone numbers were available on nurse lists, this was a very responsive market segment in the Water Quality industry.

The beauty industry, which includes hair, nail, massage and eyebrow salons, are also excellent prospects. Through the water grapevine, I've heard that some of these businesses are not as credit-worthy as we'd like them to be. Using Dun & Bradstreet, business lists can be overlaid with modeled credit to eliminate the high risk businesses and leave you with lots of great businesses to prospect.

Telemarketing is a Top Prospecting Medium in B2B

There is a big difference in how telemarketing is perceived in the work environment. Rather than an annoyance, it is an understood and expected form of lead generation / lead nurturing. But, to be effective, it takes work and most companies are biased in favor of digital channels because it feels so much easier.

But, sometimes feel doesn't cut it. Cold digital marketing is nowhere near as effective as B2B Telemarketing. Even though it takes 80 calls on average to get an opportunity, those calls will generate quality leads at a lower cost than any other method of lead generation.

Businesses who undertake a B2B Telemarketing campaign need to be prepared - using rich, top quality data, understanding that this is not a one-day event and making sure that the TSR is trained.

> *TIP:*
>
> *Want to be Successful with Telemarketing for Lead Generation? Start a Conversation. It does not have to be long, so easy and social enough to compel your audience to listen to you.*

Developing Rapport on the Phone

Many marketers have a hard time mastering the fine art of the conversation.

We are so excited when we get our prospect on the phone we tend to flood them with information. We want them to know all about our business, our offering, our Unique Value Proposition and what we can do to help them reach their goals.

Sure that will give them a lot of details, but how sure are you that they want to know that much that quickly? Truth to be told, they will most likely hang up the phone.

That's because we used a sales pitch on them. While a sales pitch is useful in guiding the conversation (and some companies insist that you follow the sales pitch verbatim), this rarely works in today's highly information-dense audience. Our prospects are deluged with information every minute of their day. Adding a zippy telemarketing sales talk will not help matters. This may cause them to resent us, close their ears and their doors, and turn your B2B lead generation campaign into a failure.

Even if the prospect is willing (and they actually need our service), they will not buy from you because you just flooded their minds with gibberish. There's got to be a better way....

The simplest, most production solution is to just start a conversation. It does not have to be long. It just has to be easy and social enough to compel your audience to listen to you. Remember, you are not telling them all the details yet. You are gauging reaction and feeling them out.

For example, your telemarketer is calling medical offices:

You: Hello, I'm (your name) from (name of your company). Is this a good time to talk?

Prospect: Yes (or No).

You: Let me make this short. We are offering a one-month free test of our super-duper new water cooler. How are you providing pure water for the patients in your waiting rooms?

This is a good conversation starter for appointment setting. The pitch does not really need to tell everything at the start, but it does set the stage for you and your team to continue the conversation. Ask them the right questions and get the information you need.

By using what you learn from this initial contact, you can then craft an effective solution to their problems. Just take it slowly and let the conversation take its course. Build rapport first and establish your relationship with them. The Master of Direct Mail Copywriting, Herschel Gordon Lewis, always talked about building rapport to create that direct mail dialogue. Building rapport on the phone works the same way.

Once you have that rapport, it becomes much easier to ask your prospect for more information so you can ask for the sale. Don't rush the process.

B2B lead generation can take several calls or conversations before the final stage is reached.

Chapter 13.

Online Lead Generation

I must get a dozen calls a week from clients or prospects who ask me for a list of people who filled out a survey on-line indicating that they are definitely interested in buying a water softener tomorrow. Oh, and by the way – it should be an exclusive lead.

C'mon gang – who are we kidding?

So where do these leads come from and how are they generated? Just like any industry – there are the good guys and the bad guys.

While there are lots of companies in the marketplace whose business is to generate leads on-line for others, much of what gets funneled down to the paying customers are the ones they haven't closed themselves or re-sell to as many companies as they can. After all, their goal is to make a profit. If you go on-line, you can read lots of horror stories about lead generation companies that lock businesses into long-term contracts and provide mediocre/duplicate/inaccurate leads.

But there are also solid on-line lead gen companies who provide decent leads. On the up-side, you may get quality leads. On the downside – you cannot count on getting a specific number of leads each week – it depends on how many people fill out the forms.

If you want to go this route and see if you can get the kind of "easy leads" you're dreaming about, before you sign up with a Lead Company for on-going service, make sure you check with the Better Business Bureau / other reviews of the site.

But the honest-to-goodness bottom line is that if you really want exclusive quality leads from an on-line source, in real time – you need to generate them yourself.

There is no one right way to generate sales leads online. Each business has a different target market and your lead generation strategy should reflect the unique aspects of your business and communicate your brand.

You need to start with your website, do all the right things in terms of backend architecture and optimization, sign up with Google Local to insure you can be found and make certain your Lead Generation Form is well designed and executed.

Create a Destination Website

While other methods can provide a more active approach to generating leads, having a website is still essential. Sure, you might have a very pretty website....but having the right features set up can help the right people find you, instead of you having to reach out to them.

Design

So many options - where to begin? Go into Wordpress.com and look at the thousands of low-cost, quality templates they offer. There are well-designed templates that have many of the bells & whistles you need for mobile compatibility and SEO indexing already built-in. You can select a template that you like, and either run with it yourself or find a developer to help you.

Remember, website development is not your business. There are people available who can get a small site up and running for under $1,000. You would not suggest that a teacher replace their own HVAC unit.

> *TIP:*
>
> *Your website needs to be search engine friendly, mobile compatible and load quickly. Double check all your company's contact information. Insure the links to your social media icons work efficiently. Your website reflects your company.*

Let's just review the Key Drivers of a solid Destination Website:

Search engine friendly site development

This means that you need make sure that all of the best practices are in-place on your site so it can be easily crawled by the Google spiders. Remember, your goal is to be found.

Mobile Compatibility

Your site needs to be mobile-compatible. Your website needs to load quickly. You need to be properly indexed so people can find what they're looking for on your site easily. Each page must be correctly named, your photos should have meta-tags; your content needs to be unique and written both for the users and for the search engines.

Loading Speed

Loading speed is vital. It's very simple to test your loading speed – Call me and I'll be happy to run a report for you.

Once you know what it is – you can easily react and take care of what you need to do to make your site load more quickly.

It might be as simple as changing the size of a photo, rethinking your sign-up form. Or you may need to rethink your hosting environment and move from a shared server, where you are sharing a certain amount of space – to a private server.

Or, try Google's self-test of your site's loading speed. It takes 30 seconds to do and it's free.

Hosting

Nowadays even small businesses can afford to have their own Virtual Private Network (VPN) – no need for a climate-controlled location or equipment like "the old days" – you just need to find the resource that's right for you. Cost for a VPN can start as low as $85/month.

People will drop your site like a hot potato if your site doesn't come up quickly – this is something you must take care of asap.

Lead Generation Form

You need to make sure you have a lead capture vehicle on every page of your website so you can acquire names/contact information of people who visit your site who express interest in your product.

Just like in direct mail, you need to create a reason for why someone would spend the time to fill out your form and give you their information. We call these Lead Magnets.

In the Water Quality market, some of the Lead Magnets used to get people to fill out on-line forms include:

- Contest Entry
- Family Size Box of Tide
- Water Safety Alerts
- E-Book Download
- Monogramed Water Bottle
- Recipes
- Water Bottle Holder

If your offer includes a free newsletter or e-book download, the digital product should relate to your paid offerings in such a way that those who download them are likely to be interested in your other services. But it should still be a quality piece that is helpful to users and can stand on its own. Once people have downloaded it, you have their information from the form. So, you can follow up with them about your other offerings.

Just like I explained when I talked about offers, people will see right through lukewarm offers. Make sure the offer you are using to entice your prospect into giving you their contact information is worthy.

The Form itself needs to be highly visible so prospects can find it. While you want your prospect to provide you with enough contact information so you can follow up with them, there is a fine line between the information you want, what the prospects is willing to provide. You may have to test several versions to see how much information a prospect in your industry will provide before they drop out of the contact form entirely. Again, it will depend on why they are completing the form and what they want to get from you as their reward for submitting it.

The Captcha

Many businesses have also found that they need to have a Captcha on the bottom of their form to insure that the forms are filled out by humans, rather than robots. There is nothing more frustrating that having a robot eat up precious marketing dollars by filling out form after form. A Captcha can eliminate this.

> **TIP:**
>
> *Use a simple Captcha. Not everyone can read skinny, waving letters and numbers and fill them in correctly. If it's too hard to deal with, people will drop the form.*

Chapter 14.

Driving Traffic to Your Website

It's not easy to be found. There are literally millions of websites in the marketplace all vying for a consumer's attention. The greatest looking, most well-written website in the world will do you no good unless people visit it.

Figuring out the best way to drive traffic to your website is huge. If you have an unlimited budget and are willing to spend thousands of dollars each month marketing your site, you will see visitors.

If you're like me, your marketing budget is limited and you have to make the most out of your dollars.

> **TIP:**
>
> *Go into Google and type in your industry into the search function. Did your company come up on top? Is it one of your competitors? Can you find yourself?*

You might want to sign up for a basic course in learning how to drive traffic to your website. There are so many options, including Search Engine Optimization (SEO), and Pay Per Click (PPC) strategies, including Google AdWords, Facebook and Linked In ads.

Many businesses also use a variety of media to drive traffic to their website, including direct mail, newspaper advertising, email marketing, as well as collateral marketing material. Everything must have your website address. Any digital media must have a live link.

Remember the Quick Response Codes (QR codes) I suggested you print on your direct mailers, ads and brochures so it can be scanned with a cell phone and link right to your site. This helps drive traffic to your site. This counts in the world of SEO

SEO – Search Engine Optimization

The SEO industry is very volatile and what was best practice in 2017 is not the same as what we will see in 2019, but the basics still hold true. You will need to develop your list of top keywords (which you can also use in Pay Per Click), create quality content, build partnerships and links with other organizations and test & tweak, using your web analytics.

There are numerous books, courses and White Papers all over the internet to give you basics of SEO. Be wary of unsolicited emails that announce that they will give you 1st page Google Ranking. There are great SEO experts in the marketplace who will work with you/coach you.

Before you can move forward, it's your job to develop a list of keywords to target

Developing Key Words and Phrases

The first step in developing a keyword list is brainstorming. Take some time and write down as many words and phrases as you can think of that relate to your site with the understanding that this is simply the start of your research. You should be able to build a list of 50 – 100 phrases without much trouble.

In 2019 – Pay Per Click is about "long-tail" keywords and phrases. Long tail keywords are those three and four keyword phrases which are very, very specific to whatever you are selling. You see, whenever a customer uses a highly specific search phrase, they tend to be looking for exactly what they are actually going to buy.

Think about what people actually type into Google and now, with the increased popularity of voice search, people are using longer and longer sentences to specify what they are looking for.

> **TIP:**
>
> *Developing your Dealership's Keywords and Phrases is a great exercise to do with your team. They may think of words and phrases you don't.*

- **Find the words and phrases your customers use.**

  Think like your prospects Figure out what they might type into the search bar in they were looking for your product. If you're selling an under the sink RO, consider a phrase like *"looking for a compact water filter"*.

- **Look for synonyms**

  Similar to the above seek the words potential clients will use. You call it *water conditioner.* They might type *water condition.*

- **Add qualifiers**

  For your Dealership, scoring high local search is vital – add your town or city in to the phrase you think your prospects will type in. A Dealership in Des Moines, Iowa might add *Des Moines, Iowa*, to almost every phrase. This will help them get in front of the more general sights.

Now, it's time to use this list of keywords or phrases in your marketing efforts and drive traffic to your website.

Pay Per Click & Targeted Ads in Social Media

Online advertising tools like Google AdWords, as well as Facebook & Linked In ads provide you with opportunities to market specific words or phrases or target the specific audience that might fit that description.

The list of keywords you created are vital for your Pay Per Click (PPC) efforts, since these are the words or phrases you want people to click on so they can find your business.

OK – here's a test. Open up Google and type in the work you do in search bar. Did you come up? Did your competitor? Can you find your business one the first page?

Google AdWords

When you look at the search results, you can see that the Google Search page is divided into Paid Search and Organic Search. In 2016, Google changed the way these are displayed and there is way more competition for real estate. If you don't see your business at the top of the page, you can pay for it, using Google AdWords. Of course, that can cost and arm and a leg, depending on the key word. Some are more costly than others, depending on the search volume.

Believe me, I would love to have first position when it comes to the word Mailing List on Google – but it would probably cost me thousands of dollars a day. That is not in my lead generation budget. Instead I use alternate/creative keywords & phrases that cost less per click. While I can't afford to market the keyword Mailing List, I can afford to market the keyword New Mover List.

It's easy to run up a huge bill with Pay Per Click Advertising. But we all know that people tend to click on what they see on top....so it becomes a function of what you can afford to spend on PPC and how you can try to end up at the top of the list organically through SEO.

Targeted Ads in Social Media

Advertising in social media is not the same thing as posting blogs and happy photos of staff in logo shirts. While it's important to show visitors to your site and social media pages that you continuously update your posts with current content and information, when we talk about advertising on the social media channels, we mean another thing entirely.

It's kind of like stalking your prospects. When they look at their Facebook page, they see your ad or sponsored post mixed in with the photos and posts from their friends. This is yet another venue for you to keep your brand and message in front of your prospect.

Facebook offers you the ability to market to their own list of Facebook customers, selecting them by age, income and interest.

You might choose to target people on Facebook, selecting people within your geographic area who have listed environmental concerns as one of their interests.

New technology allows you to creatively market to selected audiences that are not typically available through Facebook, using special matching processes to create a custom Facebook Advertising list. After all, just like with any direct marketing product, you only want to spend your dollars reaching your prime prospects.

Use What You Know & Get Creative

Based on the results of the WQA Consumer Opinion Study, you know that that 60% of New Homeowners will buy water filtration systems in the first year they are in their home. You may have reached out to them once by mail or phone and they didn't convert. Now, it's all about timing and reaching them in another way.

New Homeowner is a very valuable name.

Why not have the list of the past years' worth of New Homeowners matched and uploaded right into to your Facebook account so you can reach out to them with an on-going campaign of posts or ads?

This way you are continuing the dialogue you started when you mailed to them originally. Remember, frequency counts and people will remember your Dealership when they see your name and message in more than one medium.

Think of this as a new marketing channel for an old favorite.

> **TIP:**
>
> *Target New Homeowners with Facebook Ads. Even if they didn't buy the first time you mailed to them, it's important to keep your Dealership's name front & forward. We know that 60% of New Homeowners will buy a water filtration system in the first year they are in their new home. This is your chance to maximize every new homeowner name you can.*

Chapter 15.

Multi-Channel Marketing

Multi-Channel Marketing is a form of direct marketing that combines multiple channels such as direct mail, email, SMS (text) messages, websites, mobile apps, and Facebook advertising. With a consistent look and feel across all channels, cross-media is a powerful tool for companies to engage with their customers.

Perhaps more importantly, using multiple channels produces significantly better response rates than any one channel can on its own because it allows prospects to become involved with your Dealership on their own terms.

These are some of the benefits:

- **Increased Awareness**

  A multi-channel approach is about casting the widest net to get the maximum customer engagement.

- **Consistent Messaging**

  One benefit of multi-channel marketing is the allure of a consistent brand message. Let's go back to Culligan. And remember their well-known, highly developed slogan "Hey Culligan Man!" He was even featured on the Culligan website, print ads and TV.

- **Channel Preference**

  Reach your customers on their preferred channel. Sounds perfect, right? Yes and no. For companies with a longer buying cycle, you need to hit potential customers more than once, and that means targeting them with the right message, in the right place, at the right time within their journey. Multi-channel marketing may allow you to reach customers on the channel of their choice.

> **TIP:**
>
> *Different strokes for different folks. Not all people respond to the same marketing channels. By reaching out to prospects through multiple channels, you get your message across more efficiently.*

Mix & Match your Marketing Channels

A simple example of cross-media is a standard direct mail piece that includes a personalized URL (PURL), which the recipient of the mailer can type into a web browser or click on a QR code to view a personalized landing page. This campaign uses just two channels, print and the web. This example can be deployed for many uses including lead generation, surveys and even cleaning your own database.

Use a QR Code

A more sophisticated example would also include using the QR code on the printed mailer to take a recipient taken directly to a mobile-friendly website, so mobile is a third channel.

Using multiple channels increases the reach of your campaign it allows people to receive your message in their preferred way. We all know that some people respond better to the mail and some people are glued to their Facebook pages. By blending several marketing channels you are making it more likely that recipients will respond to your offer. This is how you can increase your response.

Nowadays many marketers are having their direct mail lists matched & uploaded right to their Facebook or Instagram ad accounts so they can blend their direct mail and social media, reaching prospects via multiple channels for extra impact. The Dealer has the ability to control his or her own Facebook or Instagram timing and spend. This means they can continue the lead generation process they started on their own terms. As I mentioned earlier, when Dealers have their New Homeowner data loaded into Facebook, they up their chances of selling them a system.

> *TIP:*
>
> *Does your Dealership have a QR code? You can download one for free at http://www.qrstuff.com/ There are also new Visual QR codes with Designs on them. You can register here for a free sample: http://www.visualead.com/login*

Chapter 16.

Social Media – Blogging, Facebook, Linked In, Twitter

You need to look at tailoring your content to a specific audience the same way you looks at targeting your ads to a particular group.

It doesn't matter if you are creating the content to encourage Homeowners to complete a form for a Free Whitepaper Download about Hydration during the Summer months or creating a newsletter directed at Psoriasis sufferers to generate interest for a soft water conditioner, the content needs to be created specifically for that group.

You want to be known as a thought leader in your industry or community. If you speak with a clear voice to a defined audience, the more the people who visit your site or read your material are actually going to be interested in what you have to offer.

Reminder – be consistent with your posts. There is no bigger turn-off than a blog or Facebook page that hasn't been updated in months.

Content is King

Content does not always have to be written from scratch. You can also curate content from other sources. Curating content is a great way to stock your blog with fresh topics and increase traffic, but as with everything in life, there is a right way and a wrong way to do it.

By carefully handpicking relevant content for your market, you can become a go-to for information. This is a great way for you to position yourself as an authority in your industry.

In terms of how this helps you generate leads for your business, this plays out by elevating your company's influence, giving you increased exposure from search engines and creating an aura of expertise in your industry.

Once you start developing and curating content – now it's time to make it work for you.

> *TIP:*
>
> *There are resources online that will help you collect and organize content. Check out Feedspot -https://www.feedspot.com/. This site will help you accumulate information in the specific topics you're interested in which will allow you to repurpose it as needed.*

Blogging

Why do we blog? We are looking to share information, increase our influence, stimulate conversation, and encourage prospects to use our service. A blog is one of the many tools in your lead generation tool box.

By using your keywords and key phrases within your blog, you can increase SEO and help drive prospects to your website. Reminder, when you blog, you need to remember that you are writing for two audiences, your prospects and the search engines.

Send out a Newsletter

Many experts believe that sending out a newsletter is an essential part of any online lead building strategy. The concept here is to catch people in their inbox.

A newsletter is a great lead generation tool. Make sure your system is set up so that when people sign up to receive your newsletter, you get a copy of their sign-up form in real time. These are great leads for your business. Plus those who are interested enough to sign up to receive your helpful content are also more likely to be interested when you update them about a new product or service you just launched.

> **TIP:**
>
> *Ask your newsletter sign-ups to White List you to insure that your newsletters will go into their inbox, not their spam box.*

Re-purposing your Content

Re-purpose your content whenever and wherever possible. Even if you created that newsletter piece for a specific target audience, you can easily re-purpose for your blog or edit it to become relevant for another audience.

Different people respond to different channels. As you become more familiar with creating, curating and re-purposing your content, you will find that some of your potential customers might be more likely to read your material in blogs or articles in LinkedIn Pulse rather than through your newsletter.

What I typically do is post my blog on the Dataman Group website, re-purpose it for Linked In Pulse and then send it out in a newsletter format to the right list group. Depending on the nature of the information, I may also send it is press release format to the Chamber of Commerce, the local Business Journal and other sites that may include it in what they offer to their membership. If the content was directed to the Water Industry, I will also include it in the Pure Water Profits blog for additional exposure directed to that specific vertical.

In addition to repurposing the content, I am also trying to maximize the visibility of the keywords and phrases I am using for additional SEO. My goal is that if someone types in one of my key phrases, the search engines will direct them to my website.

Host a Webinar

Webinars are also all about content and expertise...and they offer lots of lead generation and SEO opportunities.

First of all, just like newsletters or free downloads, people need to sign up for your Webinar. The sign up form should include enough information for you to follow up with them afterwards and add them to your newsletter list.

If you think a Webinar may be a useful tool for you, decide on a topic that would be helpful to your potential customers and then promote it on social media or online advertising.

Make sure you have the technology you need for this – there are forums like GoToMeeting or Zoom where you can sign up, send out invitations and share a direct link to your event page to interested attendees.

You can even repurpose this on Slide Share for additional SEO

Reviews & Referrals

Many businesses take an "under-promise and over-deliver" approach to their offerings and to the services they provide. Go out of your way to make your customers happy. Deliver outstanding customer service, engage them with relevant promotions and contests and treat them like people rather than customers. Never take a single customer for granted—make them believers in what you do. If those few people are excited about you, they'll share. Through sharing, commenting and linking, they'll help you spread your message.

In 2019, think 4.8 star review.

Reviews of your business really count. Consumers scrutinize and compare reviews of your company and similar businesses on the Better Business Bureau site, Google, Yelp and Facebook .Shoppers use these reviews to help them decide who to buy from as well as which companies to avoid.

Brands know that customer reviews play an integral role in consumers' purchasing decisions, especially online. As such, they work hard to drive the highest ratings they can.

There are programs you can sign up for that provide you with an easy way to get 5-star reviews on your website. (getfivestars.com)

Some consumers are skeptical of companies with all 5 star ratings (too good to be true?) and a recent study from GetApp found that product purchases were most influenced by reviews with an average star rating between 4.2 and 4.8. Having a few less-than-perfect reviews decreases a product's average star rating, but according to the study these less-than-five-star reviews that can actually be what drives purchase.

Final comment – reply to every review. If someone gave you a bad review, apologize, explain what happened and try to rectify the situation. Don't try to take down the review; that will only exacerbate someone's frustration with your company.

In terms of referrals, the reality is you don't need to convince everyone about your brand; rather, you need to find a few people who are likely to convince others for you.

Clothing subscription service, Stitch Fix, does a great job of incorporating social media into their referral strategy. Stitch

Fix uses its customer portal to encourage customers to share a referral link on the social network of their choice. Each customer gets a unique referral link, and they can earn $25 in Stitch fix rewards. You may want to try something like this for your Dealership.

Twitter

Building a network of relevant social connections doesn't happen overnight. One way to find potential leads on Twitter is by participating in Twitter chats that are relevant to your industry or target customers.

We have all seen the influence that Twitter has in the political, sports and entertainment arenas. Millions of people follow particular candidates or political figures.

As I said earlier, different people respond to different channels. I remember how excited I was when the first few people actually signed up for the Dataman Twitter feed. Nothing happens overnight and you have to work hard at building those relationships and eventually converting them into real leads.

Twitter chats can help you make those initial connections with influencers and others relevant to your industry. I have actually gotten business from some of my own tweets.

You may find Twitter a useful tool to instantaneously communicate a Boil Water notice to your twitter feed.

In any case, it's a marketing channel to experiment with.

Reach out to People in Social Groups

Some social networks such as LinkedIn and Facebook have groups that can help you connect with others in your industry or people with similar interests. These groups can be a great source for potential leads.

Make sure your bio is complete and that you have taken advantage of every opportunity to create meaningful, personal connections. Research the groups related to your business. It might not be a specific industry group, rather a group where you can do business. For example, you might join groups of retailers, new moms or home improvement professionals. Sometimes being different helps you stand out.

> *TIP:*
>
> *Remember – social media is supposed to be "social". Make it fun, make it interesting. Find articles that you can post that impact your industry. Consider using the information from the weekly WQA News Report that offers articles and links to information in your state.*

Don't "hard-pitch" your groups. Stand back and watch the conversation for a while before you jump in. Ask questions, comment, learn the group's vibe. You will need to experiment to find the groups that match your interests.

Remember to re-purpose your content in LinkedIn Pulse by sharing with your groups. You may also decide to broaden your outreach to other groups by using LinkedIn Sponsored Updates.

Partner with others and cross-promote

You've worked hard at building up a network of loyal customers. And others in your industry have done the same.

By joining forces on a project with another industry influencer, preferably one whose offerings are slightly different than your own, you both can potentially gain some new leads. A quality collaboration will enhance and elevate the importance of both of your businesses.

Bottom line, your goal is to get your brand in front of some new faces and get them to click into your site and fill out that lead generation form.

Chapter 17.

Generating Leads from Home Shows

Many Water Dealerships exhibit at live events, including Home Shows, local chamber of commerce programs, and street fairs – with an eye on generating quality leads for their salespeople to call & close.

A few quick comments

Exhibiting at Homes Shows can be stressful. With the cost of attendance, the man hours spent on planning and execution, and very real concerns about maximizing ROI, the pressure to generate quality sales leads at Home Shows is always high.

Double check your business' contact information on every piece of marketing collateral. Make sure the website is correct. Include QR codes on flyers. Select personalized giveaways that make sense with your brand.

Sarah Leung from Handshake, which is a company that specializes in increasing orders at Trade Shows, includes these suggestions to improve your Lead Generation.

Outline measurable goals

It's hard to be successful when no one has concretely defined what "success" is. The first thing to do in the planning process is to set challenging yet realistic goals for each trade show. The most important thing to consider about those goals, however, is whether they're quantifiable.

Avoid vague statements like, "we want to do better at getting people to our booth." How *much* better? How many people do you want each of your sales reps to talk to? How many leads do you want to have by the time the show's over? By setting goals that can be assessed by facts and numbers, you'll be able to measure success, as well as think of specific ways to meet those objectives.

Promote the event beforehand

It may seem strange to promote a trade show that you're not directly involved in planning. But ultimately, you have to look at that trade show as your stage, and you want as many people in the audience as possible. After all, a bigger pool of people means more potential leads.

Remember to e-blast your customers and contacts about the show. Some companies even pay for passes for their biggest buyers and/or prospects. Just make sure to let them know which booth you'll be at, so that they can make sure to stop by. Promoting a trade show will encourage attendance and your will generate leads that wouldn't have happened otherwise.

Create a unique, consistent identity for your personnel

In a sea of exhibits, it's all about how eye-catching you can be. Obviously, your booth design has a lot to do with this, but you also have the opportunity to catch people's attention with what your sales team is wearing.

Design a cool t-shirt that everyone can wear at the event. Avoid an overly promotional design, and instead go for something that will intrigue people enough to stop and see what your brand is all about.

Get interactive & Go Digital

Creating an interactive experience goes a long way toward drawing people's attention in any scenario, and trade shows are no different. By bringing in audience participation, you'll attract a crowd.

You want to create an experience around your brand and products at a trade show. The use of live demonstrations, touch screens, and interesting new technologies like mobile augmented reality are great

Attention getting techniques of doing this.

Imagine having booth visitors just point their phone screens at a product, which then triggers an animated, interactive experience. They'll remember your product–and you–for it.

With the large audience that this kind of experiential marketing brings, you'll also be able to communicate with several leads at once. Just make sure you have enough personnel on the floor to capture those leads.

Cut to the chase

Time is precious at a Home Show. There are only so many hours in each day during which you can generate those leads, so speed is paramount.

That said, avoid small talk. Both you and your attendees are there for the same purpose: business. Get straight to the point with each conversation–understanding their needs and explaining how your company can meet them.

Get complete contact information for follow up

There is nothing worse than spending all that time & money and not coming back to the office with a fistful of leads. Remember, your goal is to get as many complete contacts as possible so you can follow up by phone to close that all important in-home appointment.

> *TIP:*
>
> - *Make sure your forms are easy to complete with lots of space for information*
> - *Remember to have QR codes on all your literature to drive people to your website*
> - *Use an IPad at the booth to capture information*
> - *Consider having roving sales reps to acquire additional contacts*
> - *Take advantage of the trade shows lead capture tool that scans badges/creates contact lists*

While a Home Show environment is extremely competitive, it can also be extremely lucrative. Ultimately, you need to do whatever you can to stand out on that floor and bring home the contacts.

Once the dust settles, make sure to follow up with all of your leads as soon as possible. Be extremely quick to respond to all requests, and concentrate on setting up in-store or in-home appointments with new leads. Armed with these lead generation tips, you'll have a lot of work to do after the show is over.

Chapter 18.

Door-to-Door Lead Generation

I look at door-to-door canvassing as today's lowest cost lead generation tool.

Before businesses started generating leads via the mail or through PPC/SEO and social media, door-to-door canvassing used to be the most effective means of securing leads. People went door-to-door with products, surveys, and information about everything from political campaigns to kitchen stoves.

(I might be dating myself, but who else remembers the Fuller Brush man?)

Aaron O'Hanlon from Footbridge Media, a firm that specializes in helping home improvement contractors market, explains that "as technology made it easier to deliver the sales message and people became disenchanted with the intrusion of an uninvited guest, the popularity of door-to-door marketing declined."

What was old is new again and door-to-door canvassing has become a viable option for obtaining leads again. Now that most people have become dependent on their technology, things like social media and texting have widened the gulf between physical social interactions. A smiling face and warm, real-life conversation is a welcome change. People are now once again receptive to this type of exchange.

The benefits of door-to-door canvassing for lead generation

Coupled with other forms of advertising, door-to-door canvassing helps create brand awareness.

Meeting people in their homes creates an extremely quality lead. It is said it takes at least a couple of years before someone makes the commitment to *start* shopping for home improvement or new construction. Canvassing can shorten that to a couple of months.

> **TIP:**
>
> *If you're company is installing a Water Filtration system in a home on a given street, all their neighbors have already seen your truck. Stopping in and introducing yourself is a great opportunity to generate leads. Better yet, ask your customer for a list of their neighbors...and use their name as a referral.*

Get the jump on your competitors

For all those people out there who have started the process of shopping around, regardless of whether they have responded to someone's paid advertisements, you could sway their decision by showing up on their doorstep.

Getting to know people in your community and building relationships creates a strong referral network. Even if these people don't do business with you right away, they may become your friends and eventually lead you to people who will.

Before starting on this journey of alternative lead generation it is important to understand the two simple reasons for canvassing. First, it lowers the cost of your leads. Canvassing can be much less expensive than running print or radio ads (although you can also boost the number of leads you get when used in conjunction with those advertising channels).

Second, you can generate leads faster. When you are going door to door yourself, delivering your company or brand message, you control the flow of leads. When you need them, you can go out and get them.

> **TIP:**
>
> *The same thing works for B2B. If you are visiting a restaurant in a shopping plaza, take some time to visit other eating places in the same area. After all, you already found a parking place!*

Make Your Canvassing Efforts More Effective

- **Go in with a plan**

  Know what you want to accomplish from the encounter. Are you generating a lead, setting an appointment, doing a presentation, or just dropping off a brochure?

- **Professional Dress**

  If you look like a professional, you will be treated like a professional and more likely to have a change to get in the door.

- **Have a script**

  You don't necessarily have to memorize a spiel, but you need to have an idea of what you are going to talk about at every house. Write out an outline of your topics and some rebuttals just so you don't get stuck.

- **Be genuine and connect**

  These people will ideally become future customers. Why not start building that friendship now. People always prefer to do business with their friends anyway.

- **Put in the time**

  Canvassing, like every form of lead generation, ultimately is a numbers game. There will always be more noes than yeses. You just have to sift through all the noes to get to them.

- **Be timely**

  If your company is installing a system on a home on a given street, this is an opportunity to visit all the homes on that street. Chances are the type of chemicals in the water are the same and these neighbors need your services. They have already seen your signs and know that your company is doing a job on their street.

- **Don't get discouraged**

  You will probably never in your life experience more rejection. If you go into it with that understanding, it will be easier to deal with

- **Follow up, follow up, follow up**

You are building a relationship with these people, so it may take time, but you must follow up continuously for as long as it takes until the lead bears some kind of fruit.

- **Ask for referrals**
  It never hurts to ask.

Now is an opportune time to get an edge on your competition. Do what they aren't willing to do; go out and make some friends in your community.

It's easy. Just knock on the door and introduce yourself.

Chapter 19.

An Integrated Marketing Approach to Lead Generation

The same way I began this book by explaining that marketing for lead generation is not a single event – using only a single marketing channel is similarly doomed to fail.

That's why we talk about multi-channel marketing – believe me, your Lead Generation program will benefit from taking an integrated marketing approach to your marketing strategy.

Consumers and business people receive thousands of messages each day. You need to break through the clutter, get noticed, be remembered. Not every marketing channel resonates with every prospect. By utilizing several channels, you have a better chance that your message will be heard

When you link together your message and position your company in a consistent way across different channels, you give a broader audience a chance to recognize you and get to know your company

There is a direct correlation to the success of your company's branding and name recognition with the number of leads your company will generate. The more often people see your company's name or logo – and from different sources - the more likely they will be to keep your company in mind and the easier it will be to acquire leads.

Integrated messaging also help buyers by giving timely reminders, updated information and special offers which, when presented in a planned sequence, help them move comfortably through the stages of their buying process... and this reduces their 'misery of choice' in a complex and busy world.

Remember, you are not the only company out there communicating with prospects. It's important to use consistent images and relevant, well-thought out messages to help nurture your relationships with prospects and keep the leads coming into your sales department.

> **TIP:**
>
> *Create an Integrated Marketing Schedule so everyone in your Dealership is on the same page.*

Calendarize your marketing program. Create an Integrated Marketing Schedule for your Dealership so you know you are either reaching out to prospects or setting the stage for prospects to find you on an on-going basis. Include trade shows and community expos on your Schedule so you can market around them.

Make sure everyone on your team buys in and knows what you have scheduled. Everyone needs to be on-board because as leads flow in, you need to follow up.

Remember these effective, easy to carry-out examples of integrated marketing:

- Businesses that phone follow up a direct mailing
- Doing an email deployment in conjunction with a direct mailing
- Using linked in ads to enhance your newsletter's outreach
- Newspaper ads that coincide with a direct mailing or email deployment
- Making sure your Facebook, Google+, LinkedIn and Twitter icons are embedded in your newsletters and appear in your e-mailings.
- Promoting a Home Show with E-newsletters & direct mail
- Blending direct mail with Facebook marketing

Learn from experience.

Constantly search for the optimum communications mix. Test and tweak. Test and tweak. Your goal is to create a program where your image and messaging are reinforced as each marketing channel works together.

Chapter 20.

Marketing to the Health Conscious Consumer

Increased consumer awareness of health- and wellness-consciousness is fueling the food & beverage industry to make shifts in the way they market products.

There are many factors leading to this change including consumer awareness of health issues, greater focus on fitness, higher personal incomes, and the visibility of 24/7 news, and these factors have united to form many new markets of consumer-focused healthcare products.

Consumer healthcare is a $502 billion market that will grow nearly 50% to $737 billion over the next five years. But most interestingly, this growth will be driven primarily by preventive health and wellness products that don't require a prescription. Fueled by demand from health focused consumers, products and categories such as vitamins, nutrition, weight management, and fortified foods and beverages will see the biggest uptick.

According to a recent article by Store Brands, the baby boomer generation reportedly controls 70 percent of U.S. disposable income and drives, to a large extent, demand for healthful food & beverage products. Although the pursuit of healthy living is not unique to Boomers, it is the initiative taken by aging Boomers to create a new way of living based on the pursuit of not just *wellbeing* but *being well* that has driven permanent changes in America food culture and healthy living.

A majority of this group want more of the ingredients that have been identified to help prevent or mitigate conditions related to aging (fiber, antioxidants, vitamins and minerals, omega-3 fatty acids, vitamin D, and calcium). These enhanced nutritional needs have contributed to a robust new market shift toward functional foods and better-for-you healthcare products.

These are the trends for 2019

- Marketing towards health-conscious individuals

- Marketing 'natural' products

- Marketing preventative solutions that don't need an Rx

So, how do you position quality water as a consumer-focused better-for-you-healthcare product?

The 2017 WQA Consumer Opinion Study reports that consumers continue to be concerned about contaminants in water, food and air. The study also shows that consumers would be willing to pay for a water filtration system that removes contaminants, lead, arsenic, pharmaceuticals and biological waste.

What the study does not focus on is the basic common sense statement that in order to live a better quality life, people need to drink better quality water. The same health conscious consumer, who is concerned about the vitamins they take and the food they eat, will also be concerned about the water they drink.

TIP:

The AARP offers many articles about hydration. If your Dealership's marketing plan targets the boomer group, you may want to check out and share some of their articles with your prospects.

Identifying the health conscious consumer

These are individuals who lead a "wellness-oriented" lifestyle are concerned with nutrition, fitness, stress, and their environment. They accept responsibility for their health and are excellent customers for health-related products and services.

Dealers can buy direct mail lists of Health conscious consumers from many quality list providers who compile this data from surveys, websites, purchases and a variety of other vehicles. Telephone numbers, email address appending and Facebook matching is also available for dealers who want to market to this group using multiple marketing channels. Reaching this group through more than one marketing channel is important, for branding, impact and increased response.

In terms of messaging, it's all about health and wellness, stressing quality water as the cornerstone of living a quality life.

Kudos to Culligan Water on their new messaging initiatives. In addition to direct mail and display advertising, they are providing daily blogs and posts in a variety of social platforms featuring reasons to use Culligan water. I have seen posts that feature delicious-looking drinks to serve to friends, using

Culligan filtered water; a variety of recipes, that require Culligan filtered water; and hydration tips recommending the use of Culligan filtered water to quench even the most intense thirst.

Get the drift? Through these consistent posts, Culligan is doing a great job getting the word out on a continuous basis, building community by generating shares and re-branding themselves with their new corporate name, Culligan Water.

Can your dealership do this? It takes commitment. Remember how I started this book by saying that every Dealer needs to create their personal marketing plan? You may decide to select the three top prospect groups: New Homeowners, Families with Children and Health Conscious consumers and develop a strategy that includes a combination of direct mail, email and social media to reach them.

By utilizing multiple marketing channels and offering a combination of response mechanisms, you will be able to generate new leads for your Dealership.

> *TIP:*
>
> *Consider curating and sharing other people's posts. Click to see an example of a blog in the AARP bulletin about the benefits of cucumber water. This is where you have the opportunity to include your Dealership's information.*

Looking to the Future

Boomers are not the only market segment that is health conscious and willing to spend money to provide themselves with the best of everything. The millennial segment is also a firm believer in health and wellness and dealers need to start now to ingratiate themselves with this group, since down the road they will be the next big market for quality water systems.

The next chapter offers a deep dive into the Millennial market.

Chapter 21.

Marketing Water Filtration to Millennials

Millennials, born between 1980 – 2000 have grown up in a time of rapid change, giving them a set of priorities and expectations that differ sharply from previous generations. Their personas have been shaped by 9/11 and the 2008 financial crisis, which have impacted their belief systems and the way they view the world and themselves.

In the past year, Pew Research has revised their definition of Millennials. In the past, Millennials were judged as internet-addicted voyeurs and given very little credit for their entrepreneurial spirit. Since the original studies were done, Millennials have "aged up". More than a million millennials are becoming moms each year. They are starting families, buying homes, creating businesses and impacting their communities in a way not seen before and their mindsets continue to change with these new responsibilities.

In terms of sheer numbers, millennials are now the largest generation since the baby boomers - with over 92 million individuals; the largest generation in today's work force. They represent a population that is savvy, connected and more diverse than any previous generation.

The water industry cannot afford to neglect this group. In fact, this is the right time to nurture them and make them dedicated and loyal water filtration advocates.

We are looking at information from multiple sources in this article:

- Nielsen's report, Millennials – Breaking the Myths. This report sheds light on this diverse generation and how they consume media. Understanding the nuances of this audience is important when crafting messages and developing a marketing mix that gains traction.
- 2017 WQA Consumer Opinion Study, conducted by the Water Quality Association and released at this past WQA Conference. This study contains concrete information about buyers of water filtration systems. Click here for the summary & highlights of the Study.
- Goldman Sachs – Data Story: Millennials Coming of Age

- BCG Perspectives - How Millennials Are Changing the Face of Marketing Forever
- Pew Research Reports on Millennials

Here are some of the findings from these reports:

Millennials care about their well-being

When Chipotle announced that they would no longer use genetically-modified ingredients, social media exploded with millennial enthusiasm. Millennials are dedicated to wellness, devoting time and money to exercising and eating right. Their active lifestyle influences trends in everything from food and drink to fashion. They're using apps to track training data and online information to find the healthiest foods.

Millennials are Image-Conscious

Millennials are image-conscious consumers, which could be a natural byproduct of growing up among constant exposure on social media. To many millennials, the simple act of selecting a beverage during a lunch break is the potential for a statement about their identity and values. In fact, half of millennials believe that brands "say something" about "how they fit in" to the world as a whole, and 59% are willing to pay more for a brand that portrays the right image.

Millennials are Green

Pew Research on millennials in adulthood indicates that while less than a third of millennials identify as outright environmentalists, they're the most "sustainable" generation to date. Young adults are:

- More likely to support strict environmental policies and regulations
- 80% prefer to work for sustainable employers
- Choose sustainable transportation options when possible
- Will pay more for eco-friendly products

Regardless of how millennials perceive the label of "environmentalist," it's clear that many members of this age group behave in ways that are clearly sustainable. This includes considering a product's potential environmental impact when making purchase decisions and forming loyalties.

Millennials are Driving Sustainable Packaging Trends

Millennials view taking care of themselves and the planet as one and the same. This group's preference for healthy, convenient foods, packaged sustainably have had a significant impact on the packaging industry.

There was a fascinating case study by a company called Tetra Pak which examined declines in prepared soup consumption and how they suddenly reversed. It's all related to the recent availability of biodegradable packaging, or the paper cartons of soup that have become so common. 75% of millennials prefer soup in paper cartons to cans. While many of these consumers might not be aware that paper cartons are 70% more eco-friendly than cans, the visible sustainability of millennial-targeted soup packaging has made a clear impact.

Think about Water in a Box – It's marketed as "Natural mineral water that's cleansed, filtered and nestled deep in the Earth's foundations. Packaging that's a recyclable Box made from low carbon, light weight, naturally renewable and recyclable materials that are sourced responsibly".

The company' mantra *"This is a Movement, not a fad!"* resonates with millennial thinking.

Millennials as consumers

In light of these statistics, it's important to take into account how these millennials are consuming media. While millennials tend to choose brands that resonate with them, millennials also trust their peers and celebrities. The millennial generation wants to be a part of a larger conversation. They want to make individual contributions and be connected and woven into a larger discussion.

Millennials *prefer to do business* with *corporations* and brands with pro-social messages, *sustainable* manufacturing methods and ethical *business* standards.

With unlimited product information at their digital fingertips, millennials are turning to brands that can offer maximum convenience and sustainability at the lowest cost.

Millennial Females - Typically Bottled Water Users Today

The 2017 WQA Consumer Study points out that millennial females are typically bottled water users. For her, it's all about convenience, lifestyle and efficiency.

> *TIP:*
>
> *The bottled water industry has made water into a fashion statement. How can you feature your filtered water being used as a fashion accessory?*

While the millennial female may be a dedicated bottled water drinker today, as millennials enter the housing market and begin to start families, the dynamics will change. There is a huge opportunity with this key group and the industry needs to start to craft the marketing message now.

Crafting the Message for the Future

The message needs to appeal on multiple levels – informational, social, convenience, price, social responsibility and sustainability.

In terms of marketing channels, marketers must need to diversify the marketing mix and incorporate multiple touch points, so their message is reached via the different channels. A recent USPS study indicated that 77% of millennials enjoy and read their direct mail. While millennials may be very tech savvy, they still look forward to and read their mail.

Millennials make decisions based on a lot of information gathering, including on line reviews and recommendations by friends. It's important to focus on providing quality information about the importance of pure water for health; how many glasses of water a day are necessary for a healthy lifestyle; details on how pure, filtered water provides muscles with energy; Share statistics on how many liters of water is necessary for every 15 minutes of activity; How water is important for radiant skin. Dealer blogs might also include eating tips, making healthy deserts from summer fruits.

Millennials are Social; they enjoy the companionship of others. Your messaging need to focus on the social aspect of enjoying good tasting water with friends. Photos may include a group of friends sitting around the pool, drinking water with sliced fruit in it from cool glasses. A blog may showcase using fruit or edible flowers to make unique ice cubes. Or post a You-Tube video on how to use the mold to make the special big ice cube for scotch. Or depict a couple at home enjoying quality coffee made with quality water.

TIP:

Great visuals really count. Make sure your photos are compelling and inviting. Millennials will share photos they are attracted to with their friends and cohorts. There are resources online offering access to fabulous photos for free.

Check out Pexels - https://www.pexels.com/ and Unsplash - https://unsplash.com/ for free photo downloads.

The BCG Study indicates that convenience and 24/7 availability was rated as one of the 3 top reasons for choosing a brand. Millennials can enjoy quality water 24 hours a day, 7 days a week, from a home water filtration system. The industry also needs to focus on comparing the cost and sustainability of a filtered water system versus the cost of buying bottled water.

Price. While findings from the 2017 WQA Consumer Study indicate that the price of bottled water has had little impact on the decision to purchase alternatives, as this huge cohort takes on home ownership and the costs associated with it, one of the keys will be focusing on the smart investment of a water filtration system.

Millennials are also very price conscious with many having student loan debt. This does not mean that Millennials are not buying. They are exploring new ways to purchase the items they want in a financially responsible way. Some are choosing new financing options that allow them to buy an item now and spread out their payments over several months, all while avoiding compounding interest and hidden fees. Millennials are trying these new financing innovations they believe help them maintain greater control over their financial health.

Social Responsibility and Sustainability. Millennials placed tremendous importance on the causes a brand supports. Millennials love Starbucks and Bombas Socks because of their values and social commitment.

Interestingly, according to the WQA Consumer Study, the Green Movement has had little impact to date on the decision to purchase bottled water. 83% of respondents answered that the green movement has had no impact on an individual's decision to purchase bottled water.

However, as millennials become home owners and stakeholders in their communities, they will start to rethink bottled water purchases, because they can now have a convenient, low-cost alternative in their homes. We will also begin to see millennials gravitating to trendy re-useable water bottles that they can show off to their peers when they go to exercise class or drop off their children at pre-school. Now that they are having children, their environmental worldview will also begin to change as they look towards a sustaining future for their children.

Different Style of Marketing Engagement

In marketing, calls to action need to inspire engagement, rather than robotic consumption. For millennials, editorial content that is valuable and sharable may be more effective than traditional advertising. It's not only about winning over millennials so that they buy a system, we need to convert the female millennial into an advocate for in-home filtered water who espouses the benefits to her peers.

Websites need to be agile, mobile-friendly and offer a review module that enables users to see public reviews of your products and services and post their own reviews to share with others.

Be authentic. Millennials distrust traditional advertising, so avoid hard-sell language. Use a straightforward, transparent approach.

Use enhancements such as scent, sound, or texture to make your piece stand out.

Incorporate multimedia and digital: Embed QR Codes, barcodes, near field communication (NFC), or augmented reality (AR) to link your mailer to video and interactive materials on your website or social media sites.

Make sure you offer compelling photos, stories and solid content. Be part of the larger world of water and make your dealership look larger than it is.

Help them feel good about their purchase. Millennials are compassionate and want to improve their world. Campaigns that donate a percentage of profits to a worthy cause or in some other way demonstrate corporate responsibility can resonate—if they're seen as authentic.

Your marketing strategy needs to provide millennials with opportunities to take control of their well-being, build relationships with your dealership, make it easy to share information and photos and start a genuine conversation about health and sustainability for themselves, their families and the planet.

Chapter 22.

Marketing Water Quality Products to Women

Does your marketing resonate with women? Are you using then right messaging; the right marketing channels for success?

Women control more than 85% of all the discretionary income in the U.S – over $7 trillion dollars. They are your audience. If your targeting and messaging is not on point, they will toss your direct mailer into the trash or delete your message from their inbox without even a glance.

Women are the decision makers in the household, especially when it comes to a product that will enhance the health and wellness of her family. A mother's goal is to protect her children at all costs. And, when it comes to some of the reasons of why use a filtration system or softener, the industry has traditionally, and appropriately, targeted the female of the household.

With today's segmentation technology you can target images and copy to each person on your list differently within the same mailing, whether it be print or digital. Regardless of channel, your messaging needs to be seamless.

Top considerations when marketing to women:

1. Emotion — Research has shown that women score higher on emotional intelligence or empathy tests than men**. Since women process incoming information with emotion, if your marketing message has no emotional component, it will be ignored.

While facts and statistics are important, they are not as well-remembered as emotion. The Gender Emotion Study also points out that disgust and fear are the emotions that have the highest reaction. Did you ever see the ASPCA TV ads showing emaciated dogs in terrible conditions? I hate these ads, they upset me. But the truth of the matter is that those ads get the highest response of any fundraising ad on TV.

While we do not advocate marketing water filtration products using fear, there are ways you can subtly take advantage of this and make your messaging tap into these two emotions.

An example would be to emphasize a mother's concern about children absorbing contaminants from fertilizer run-off in the local water supply as her motivator for finding a healthful solution for her household.

2. Focus on the Big Picture — Women typically take a more holistic approach to life. Emphasize why your filtration system will not only make her life better but, at the same time, will help save our planet Earth and make a brighter future for our children.

We know from the WQA Consumer Opinion Study that focusing on the environment as a standalone reason to buy a system does not resonate with the public. However, using the environment as an adjunct reason will enhance the benefits your system provides.

Reach out to women with well-rounded messaging. Explain how your system helps improve her whole life by giving her more time, better health, and a better future for the family.

Example:

Not only does using a water filtration system offer your family clean, clear water to drink but, at the same time, helps eliminate plastic bottles, offers 24/7 convenience, saves money and conserves energy. Not to mention that it also saves you from serious back pain lugging cases of water from the store to the car and into the house.

3. Storytelling — There really is a big difference in the way marketing is perceived between men and women. Women prefer a more nuanced and storied approach, where men prefer direct-and-to-the-point messages. Keep in mind that women buy the majority of all products and services, so how do you craft your messaging to resonate with them?

Women appreciate stories that offer a capacity for empathy. By using well-told stories, images and authentic characters, you can craft a compelling story that drives response.

Your story needs to captivate your readers by engrossing them in the challenge   inherent in the story. There needs to be a clear sense of progress and contrast from the "before" state to the "after" state. Make sure to highlight your dealership's role in this transformation—after all, you are selling your company's ability to make a difference.

> **TIP:**
>
> *You can show a hostess' embarrassment at seeing ugly rust stains on her sidewalk when guests come to visit and her delight in welcoming friends into her home in front of a stain-free sidewalk after her new water softener was installed.*

Do you remember the video clip from Curb Your Enthusiasm criticizing the hostess of a dinner party for serving unfiltered tap water at the table? Click HERE to cringe and watch.

4. Safety & Security - Women need to feel comfortable with the people coming into their homes. Well pressed, logo'd uniforms convey professionalism. Visible photo ID is a must. Women are more likely to trust someone who they know is licensed, bonded, insured and WQA certified.

Here's an idea: What about sending a text with the technician's name and photo before he arrives at the home? This type of message is very reassuring. She now knows exactly who will be coming into her home, can recognize him at the door and feel confident that this person is safe. This also acts as another level of confirmation for her in terms of timing. No woman wants to hang around waiting for sales or service personnel to show up.

This is also the kind of great customer service that women will want to share with her friends.

5. Social Networking — Women are extremely social. Look for ways you can tap into that with online strategies, including social media groups and communities. This is where your posting and blogging skills will come in handy.

Portray your dealership as professional and efficient and your staff as human and likeable. People want to do business with businesses they admire and people they like.

Make sure you have a visible presence in the community. Participate in local events, sponsor a little league team, donate to the local church fundraiser, speak at the PTA.

Be visible during emergency situations. Hand out branded bottled water.

Consider creating a rewarding referral program. Women can be your best brand ambassadors.

6. Reputation — Women of all ages are equally likely to check online customer reviews and browse products online before making purchases.

Is the Reviews section on your website current? We all know that a negative review online can seriously damage your reputation. Are you following best practices for   handling reviews?

Women have a large network of people who they discuss things with. A negative experience will reverberate and be passed along to her off-line network at work, car pool or at church. Remember the game "telephone"? By the time a bad experience gets passed along the network, it has morphed into something much worse than it was.

Make sure you deliver on what you promise. Take care of any issues promptly.

Thank your new customers quickly. A good thank you is remembered warmly. That's the buzz you want to create.

7. The Right Offer — Women really love a deal. Make her decision easy to make by providing a really good offer. A good offer is not necessarily about discounting price, it's about providing something that will help clinch the appointment or actually close the sale.

Your offer cannot be lukewarm or boring. This is your call to action. People don't take action if they're not inspired.

Consider giving out a monogrammed water pitcher for the table or offering a "buy a system, get a designer drinking water faucet for free". Many dealers have done well offering a free family-sized Tide.

The word "free" is a powerful driver of response.

8. Price — Price cannot be the product driver. It's way too easy to go on-line and compare prices to find the cheapest option. Fortunately, women do not always purchase on price, they purchase based on value.

To her, your Dealership's value stems from its' sterling reputation, the attention to detail on your website and in your marketing materials, your excellent offer and the quality of your in-home appointment. If you score well on all these points, your prospect will be willing to pay more to you than the other company whose rep showed up at her house an hour late in scruffy jeans.

When marketing to women, always remember that it's not about the features of the system – it's about the benefits of the system. Your goal is to show her how absolutely indispensable your system is to her family's health and her quality of life. If you have made your case and truly presented the benefits of your system, price becomes a secondary conversation.

9. Authenticity — Women require authenticity. You must be honest and straightforward in all your marketing. Women are intuitive and can detect an imposter right away. She will avoid your product or service and tell others to as well.

As far as marketing channels, direct mail is considered the most trustworthy form of marketing. Water quality dealerships who intelligently craft their images and massaging have been successfully using direct mail for a long time.

This year, consider including the USPS Informed Delivery program into your marketing mix. This not only increases your exposure, but raises your brand awareness.

With Informed Delivery, an image of your physical mail is emailed to your prospect.

Statistic shows that 65% of users actively look at their daily Informed Delivery emails, which is way, way above the typical response rate for basic email. These emails also come from a trusted source, which adds credibility to your marketing campaign.

Today's enhanced targeting ability gives you a new edge to reaching women with a message geared especially for them. Doing a better job engaging with women is the way to increase your marketing response and grow your Dealership

Chapter 23.

How Larry David Reshaped the Way Americans View Tap water

The taste of tap water was a common thread in the 2017 episodes of Curb Your Enthusiasm, especially the episode called "How to Filter Yourself". Any self-respecting hostess who is even thinking of serving tap water to her guests should watch the clip.

Want to watch it right now? Click here.

From a water quality perspective, one of the most important pieces of this phenomenon was that we were talking about taste – not bacteria, not lead – but simply the taste of the water.

The Water Quality Industry could not have asked for a better gift. This Curb Your Enthusiasm clip became water cooler talk and people at dinner parties started to question the water they were being served. Tap or filtered? That became a real topic of conversation.

BTW – we have another great clip for your entertainment, The Water Taste Test. If you ask Jeff, Larry David is a genius when it comes to identifying water brands in a blind taste test. Want to watch it right now? Click here.

TIP:

The question of tap or filtered is also prevalent at restaurants. Customers get peeved when restaurants serve poor tasting tap water, forcing them to buy fancy, high-priced bottled water. Don't forget to market Water Filtration Systems to restaurants!

Chapter 24.

Putting it all Together with Engagement Marketing

The marketing people want to create relationships; salespeople just want to close the sale.

Consumers have so many more choices than ever before. There is tremendous competition in the water quality market and many products and services offer similar features. People shop on-line to get the best price and expect you to match it. The end result of all this is that it gets harder and harder to close that sale based simply on product features and price.

To move past this, today's marketing needs to build relationships that override basic features and price. In the old days, we called that building rapport. Nowadays, we call it building engagement.

Unlike traditional approaches to marketing where you specifically target prospects with a direct response offers to convert the sale and sell them a system, engagement marketing allows your audience and potential customers to interact with you, shape how they would like to communicate and develop a relationship.

The overriding concept is that people will buy a system from you because they trust you. And how do they learn to trust you? Through engagement marketing.

With engagement marketing, you are creating that trust by driving your interested audience towards these goals:

- Encouraging a dialogue with the individual to help them to make a purchase decision. An engaged customer is likely to become a loyal repeat customer.

- Cultivating the individual as an advocate of your thought leadership and market image. You want to develop a cadre of advocates will recommend your dealership enthusiastically to their network of friends and business colleagues.

Here are the 10 easy tips on engagement marketing to attract customers and build their trust:

1. **Develop an Engagement Plan** – To be successful, you need to start with a clear strategy, plan and approach for your engagement marketing. Your plan will have to include how you will reach out to your audience, which media you will use and how you will be able to respond and interact with your engaged participants.

2. **Integrate with your marketing mix** – All aspects of your marketing communications need to blend together seamlessly, which is why your Engagement Plan is so important. Every outreach in your arsenal needs to include a 'call to action' for engagement. Use direct mail, email, social media and even telemarketing, where it's appropriate for your outreach. Try to move your audience from one marketing channel to another to increase engagement.

3. **Focus on content and relationship** – Your audience needs to feel that you are providing them with information they can't get from anyone else. That's why they are hanging on your every word! Building genuine relationships by providing great content that is important to the individual is the best way to achieving

the two key goals of engagement marketing creating loyalty and being the expert.

4. **Become a thought leader** – Expand your reach by becoming a guest blogger or commentator on other sites. Consider writing articles for trade magazines or speaking about water quality at the local chamber of commerce or PTA. These actions give you more credibility and opportunity for additional interactions.

5. **Grow Your List** – Use permission based techniques to encourage subscriptions to your own email list so you can reach out to customers and prospects via email, phone or direct mail. Ways to do this may include contest entries, subscription registration, water testing & bottle drops or using a lead magnet to drive interest. Then, add look-alikes to your list, using rented prospect lists for both mail and electronic marketing.

6. **Invite listeners to interact with your Blog** – Establish a culture and enthusiasm for engagement by encouraging your audience to contribute with comments and suggestions to your blogs and posts. This helps them connect with you even further...and their comments get broadcast to their network, which

further increases your reach with their connected communities.

7. **Conduct surveys and polls** – Run surveys from time to time to give your customers and prospect audiences opportunities to tell you what they think. This is another way to initiate engagement to learning from and about your listening community. Use a surveys or web polls to start the dialogue that is relevant to the individual.

8. **Engage with social networking on the social networking sites –** For B2B, use linked in. If your goal is to attract consumers, try Facebook and Instagram. If you're looking for a younger consumer segment, consider Snapchat. Remember, in social networking, you are not hard-selling, rather engaging with people in their own interest areas, with the goal that they share your content with their own networks. BTW – the Larry David clip I emailed to my social networks in the water industry were shared hundreds of times, which broadened my outreach in the industry tremendously.

9. **Marketing on social sites** – Marketing on the social sites is not the same as networking and posting puppy pictures. This is your opportunity to boost your

outreach to look-alike audiences and start the engagement process on the social media sites using sponsored posts and ads.

10. After the sale – Encourage customers to give you great reviews on your products and services and share those reviews with their networks.

Remember, once you have an interested community engaging with you, make sure you keep the lines of communication going. This way you can learn and adjust your strategy to ensure your engagement marketing will deliver bottom-line results to your business by increasing your customer base and repeat sales from your engaged customers.

Make them trust you. And then they will buy from you.

Chapter 24.

Epilogue

Like you, my company is a small business. We market the products and services we provide through multiple channels and developing an amazing engagement strategy for clients and prospects is my goal for 2019

My goal is to get to the top of the Google search list with a well-rounded SEO program, that includes all the basics, including developing & posting content for newsletters, blogs and articles, participating in social media, cultivating partnerships with other companies and building a network of solid backlinks that prospects will click on.

At Dataman Group, each year, we review our results from our own marketing efforts and create new goals for the coming year.

This past year, we updated our website into a widescreen look with all the bells and whistles, including multiple lead generation forms, a new chat feature, an improved on-line count and order system, and an upgraded reviews section. As I always say, you need to give people a chance to reach you however they want. Prospects and customers can reach us by phone, form, chat or review.

We also enhanced the WaterProspects.com section of the site to make it easier for our Dealers to find what they want and need. Please visit it and let me know what you think.

On the back-end of my site, I continuously review and update my title tags and meta descriptions to improve our SEO. I have also done a lot to make our site more mobile-friendly, since mobile has become a larger percentage of our website visitors. It's imperative that our pages load quickly and I have invested the time and technology to do that.

I have added prospect direct mail back into my marketing budget, using some real out-of-the-box pieces that stand out in the mailbox. My goal is to use the direct mail to drive people to our site and to our phones.

We also hired a telemarketer for lead generation. She calls prospects, old customers, and follows up on leads we haven't closed. Even though it took a little longer than I would have liked to get this program rolling efficiently, we are thrilled with the results. It's just a fact - any new direct marketing initiative requires testing and tweaking until you get it right.

We all have to keep up with the newest trends so we can continue to stay relevant to our audience. Our content drives our relevancy to prospects, customers and to the world of search.

I will continue to reach out to all of you by direct mail, through the phone, via our monthly Constant Contact email blasts, through LinkedIn, with relevant blog posts, articles in industry publications, and even a book written specifically for you, our valued clients in the Water Quality Industry.

Your success is our success. May we all continue to work together and build strong profitable businesses for many years to come.

DALE "DataDale" FILHABER

Dale "DataDale" Filhaber is President & Listologist Supreme of Dataman Group Direct, a Florida-based direct marketing company founded in 1981.

DataDale is a well-known author, lecturer and direct marketing commentator. In the past 30+ years, she has trained many water quality dealers in direct marketing and lead generation techniques, ranging from direct mail to telemarketing to social media.

DataDale has published many articles in Water Conditioning Products and Water Technology magazines & is the author of Pure Water Profits, a blog on marketing for the water quality industry. She is a Water Quality Association member and a frequent guest lecturer at annual WQA conferences.

"Lead Generation for Water Quality Dealers – 2019 edition"' is DataDale's fourth book. This new book focuses on giving Dealers, marketing directors and sales managers the latest tools they need to develop an integrated marketing program to boost the number of leads they bring into their dealerships.

First released in 2017, "Lead Generation for Water Quality Dealers" was heralded as a must read for water dealers. Her first book, "Lead Generation Made Easier", has generated over 1,000 downloads.

DataDale can be reached at dale@datamangroup.com

DATAMAN GROUP DIRECT

The team at Dataman Group Direct has been providing lead generation data for Water Quality Dealerships for over 30 years. The company was originally known for the Dataman New Homeowner list, which has become the backbone of every Dealer's marketing program.

Dataman Group offers a myriad of lists geared to generate leads at every Dealership, including New Homeowners, Parents of new Babies, Homeowners with Children, Ailment Sufferers, Health-Conscious Consumers, Eco-Conscious Homeowners, Women, Millennials, Pet Owners and Businesses as well as Homeowners with Modeled Credit.

Dataman Group also helps Dealers analyze their customer lists and append telephone numbers, e-mail addresses and cell phone numbers to their data, creating multi-taskable lists for a blended omni-channel marketing experience.

Dataman Group Direct is committed to the Water Quality Industry and the Water Quality Research Foundation.

Dealers and marketing managers are invited to visit Dataman Group's specialized website, www.waterprospects.com, which is dedicated to providing industry-specific information, expert marketing tips and an on-going source of lead generation training tools.

The Dataman Group Team can be reached at (800) 771-3282

www.ingramcontent.com/pod-product-compliance
Lightning Source LLC
Chambersburg PA
CBHW080959170526
45158CB00010B/2842